BLUEPRINT FOR A HACK

LEVERAGING INFORMAL BUILDING PRACTICES

VIKRAM BHATT
DAVID HARLANDER
SUSANE HAVELKA

HACK

Available Resources: culverts, crates, tires, tanks, barrels, sea cans, car parts and palettes are common building materials readily available in the Canadian North.

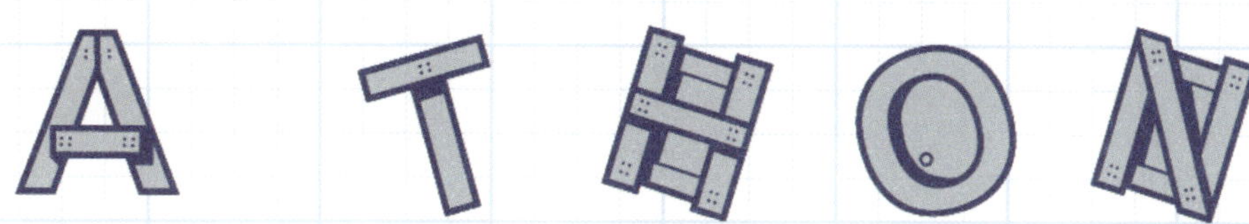
ATHON

BLUEPRINT FOR A HACK
LEVERAGING INFORMAL BUILDING PRACTICES

AUTHORS

Vikram Bhatt
David Harlander
Susane Havelka

BOOK DESIGN

David Harlander
Susane Havelka

COPY EDITOR

Jeff Cossette

COVER

Elevation and plan of the Hackathon pavilion. Drawings: Justin Bouttell and David Harlander.

KUUJJUAQ HACKATHON TEAM

Project Leads
Vikram Bhatt
David Harlander
Susane Havelka

Partners
Tunu Napartuk
Marie-Pierre McDonald

Coordinators
Ron Gordon
David Harlander

Design
Vikram Bhatt
Kassandra Bonneville
Justin Bouttell
Maggie Cabana
Andrée-Anne Caron-Boisvert
David Harlander
Susane Havelka
Emmanuelle Lauzier
Alexandre Morin
Flavie Martineau
Mae Ningiuruvik
Paul Parsons

PROJECT FUNDING

Habiter le Nord Quebecois / Living in Northern Quebec (a SSHRC-funded research project)

The Northern Village of Kuujjuaq

Peter Guo-Hua Fu School of Architecture and Faculty of Engineering
McGill University

Groupe BC2

The Canadian Centre for Architecture

The Conseil des arts et des lettres du Québec

WEBSITES

www.facebook.com/nunavikhackathon
www.mchg.ca/hackathon

PUBLISHER

Actar Publishers
New York, Barcelona

PRINTING AND BINDING

Arlequin

DISTRIBUTION

Actar D, Inc. New York, Barcelona.

New York
440 Park Avenue South, 17th Floor
New York, NY 10016, USA
T +1 2129662207
E salesnewyork@actar-d.com

Barcelona
Roca i Batlle 2-4
08023 Barcelona, Spain
T +34 933 282 183
E eurosales@actar-d.com

INDEXING

English ISBN: 978-1-948765-41-1
PCN: Library of Congress Control Number: 2019951128

Publication date: 2020

SPECIAL THANKS

The Kuujjuaq Hackathon, on which this book is based, was a complex undertaking that was made possible by the generous support of several institutions and many individuals. Our special thanks to the Northern Village of Kuujjuaq, the Kativik Regional Government (KRG), the Kativik Municipal Housing Bureau (KMHB), the Jaanimmarik School, the Pitakallak elementary school and the municipal dump for their support and collaboration in the project.

To the Living in Northern Quebec / Habiter le Nord Québécois (HLNQ) research group, McGill University's Peter Guo-hua Fu School of Architecture and The Canadian Centre for Architecture, for recognizing the importance of community-based design work and providing financial support for the project.

To the Royal Architectural Institute of Canada, the Canadian Institute of Planners, and the Canadian Society of Landscape Architects for helping to bring national attention to the project by awarding it the 2018 National Urban Design Award in the Small or Medium Community Urban Design category.

To Jim Nicell, Dean of the Faculty of Engineering and Martin Bressani, Director Peter Guo-Hua Fu School of Architecture, McGill, for their interest and support for the project.

Our gratitude also extends to Helina Gebremedhen (Curatorial Coordinator) Giovana Borasi (Chief Curator) and Mirko Zardini (Director) at the CCA, who devoted so much time and talent in organizing the 2016 Reassembling the North design charrette.

Special thanks goes out to many individuals from Kuujjuaq including, Paul Parsons, Tunu Napartuq, Steeven Gosselin, Ron Gordon, Véronique Gilbert, Gina Jean, Richard Ayangma Koko, Chantal Lalonde, Martin Lévesque, Frédéric Massicotte, Maxime Paquet, Marianne Ricard, Lisa Smith, and Charlie Watt. We are very thankful to Geneviève Vachon at 'Habiter le Nord Québécois' for her timely participation at critical points of the project and her ongoing support.

We also would like to thank Marie-Pierre McDonald whose insight from many years of working in Kuujjuaq as a land-use planner, was instrumental to the success of the project.

Finally, we also owe a very special thanks to the entire project design-build team; Kassandra Bonneville, André-Anne Caron-Boisvert, Justin Bouttell, Maggie Cabana, Emmanuelle Lauzier, Flavie Martineau and Alexandre Morin for their incredible energy and dedication to the project.

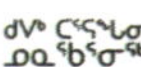

Remote resourcefulness.

In-between space.

Hacking trash / The Kuujjuaq Hackathon.

CONTENTS

Foreword: LEARNING FROM THE NORTH

In recent years, attention has been refocused on the Northern Territories in Canada, as climate change and a shifting geopolitical landscape have renewed reflections and research on the region, folding it back into the center of current discourse. The present moment for the North, while distinct, is still deeply informed by its past of military intervention, when the region was strategically used to monitor potential missile attacks as tensions escalated during the Cold War; or one of resource extraction through the mining and the building of oil pipelines, an issue that still persists. Canada's North was and is an area where new infrastructure can be laid unencumbered by strict regulations or sensitivity to local indigenous cultures and the environment – its past misgivings still inform its present.

A larger effort now exists to address the repercussions of past actions and to decouple Canada from images of pristine landscapes and acts of altruism, in order to productively confront chronic systemic issues which have affected the most vulnerable groups and environments.

A *Blueprint for a Hack* is most revealing in recognizing towns that exist at the periphery of global networks; the geographic remoteness of the North impedes its ability to fully participate in these global systems. Exporting waste to other regions of the world, a common practice among first world countries, is not a feasible option for communities based in the North. Our modern relationship with waste, predicated on its disappearance from everyday encounters, is subverted. Instead, the consequences of engaging in these systems based on consumption are laid bare, rendering visible the amount of waste that is produced, often with landfills located in or on town's fringes.

The CCA has a deep interest in issues of the environment and in understanding the migration of an idea to the specificity of a locale, where it is manifest within the built environment. These issues have been explored in a number of projects such as: *Environ(ne)ment* (2006), *1973: Sorry, Out of Gas* (2007), *Journeys* (2010), and *It's All Happening So Fast* (2016). The CCA's support of the *Reassembling the North* Charette, and *The Kuujjuaq Hackathon*, is one way it continues to stoke, interrogate, and expand these areas of thought.

Blueprint for a Hack intersects two critical issues facing the region: waste management and the need for community infrastructure in the North. Architecture operates as a new framework for putting these two problems into conversation, to offer a more nuanced response to the region's distinct cultural and environmental context. This project picks up lines of thinking and inquiry as exhibited by the research unit, The Minimum Cost Housing Group based in McGill University, which have focused on the "human settlement problem of the poor," in both developing and developed countries: Argentina, Sri Lanka, Uganda, Philippines, Mexico, Nigeria, India, China, and Canada. The role of architecture is understood in respect to the larger cultural sphere and informal building practices that, when designed for a particular region, can assuage certain needs and pressures. The imperative for these interventions' points to a changing relationship with our modern environment that can be understood as a series of responses to man-made crises, with a continuous call to manage these disturbances.

Mirko Zardini, Director
Canadian Centre for Architecture (CCA)

A view of Inukjuak with fog. *Inukjuak, QC*, 2017.

INTRODUCTION

With new materials on site – the team prepares for construction. *Kuujjuaq, QC*, 2017.

Disassembling plywood crates.
Kuujjuaq, QC. 2017.

Preparing materials for construction.
Kuujjuaq, QC. 2017.

Preparing tire foundations.
Kuujjuaq, QC. 2017.

The space between the Kuujjuaq ice rink and village's baseball diamond. *Kuujjuaq, QC*. 2017.

ARCTIC URBANISM: A CROSS-CULTURAL EXPERIENCE

Set upon a vast, isolated land, Inuit perception of time and space is markedly different from that of southern Canadians. Influenced by symbolic narratives conveyed through oral tradition, Inuit understanding of the landscape is at once spiritual and practical, a synthesis that let generations master the world's harshest environment. For the once nomadic Nunavik Inuit, the concept of boundaries, much less the administrative or legal kind, is a vague curiosity. Still, the municipal system forced them to mark their territory, defining orientations and land use with an alien logic of spatial division (Collingnon,1996). The sum of this calculation, meant to control, is invalid in an era of profound cultural, technological and social transformation. When collaborating with Inuit communities on development projects, urban planners must be particularly attentive to the point of view, needs and demands of those communities in order to develop projects that meet functional requirements without sacrificing local values, culture, traditions, lifestyles and aspirations. The participatory dimension of the process is essential and will continue to be so they can grasp this change. The Nunavik Hackathon challenges status quo thinking about northern urban design practices. Its participatory design/build approach – inclusive, flexible, and practical – offers a new methodological basis for development projects. Clearly, planners who account for the singular needs and capabilities of local stakeholders can build projects that not only surpass functional requirements but become monuments of change. BC2 was proud to be part of the Nunavik Hackathon and sincerely congratulates each participant for their amazing contribution.

Debarbieux, Bernard. "Béatrice COLLIGNON, Les Inuit: ce qu´ ils savent du territoire, Paris, L´ Harmattan, 1996, 254 pages." *Cybergeo: European Journal of Geography* (1998).

Olivier Perron-Collins
President, BC2

Marie-Pierre McDonald
Indigenous Collaboration, BC2

Playing on the table-top. *Kuujjuaq, QC*, 2017.

A CASE FOR A HACKING MINDSET
UNE CAS POUR UN MENTALITÉ PIRATAGE

In the fall of 2017, a group of young Inuit joined a team of designers from southern Quebec to reimagine underused public spaces in the Northern Village of Kuujjuaq. Making use of a vibrant and resourceful Arctic building culture, the Kuujjuaq Hackathon, a five-day design build event, demonstrated how limited resources can be a design inspiration and how communities can put the "social" back in public space.

Blueprint for a Hack documents the event, highlighting critical elements of a successful hacking methodology that can inform future planning and design practices. While focused on a remote northern Canadian community's response to conventional practices, its methods have far-reaching implications that begin to address global concerns related to design and patterns of material consumption as well as a growing need to advance innovative collaborative approaches to planning and urban design.

À l'automne 2017, un groupe de jeune Inuit s'est joint à une équipe de concepteurs du sud du Québec pour réinventer des espaces publics sous-utilisés dans la petite ville de Kuujjuaq. S'appuyant sur une culture de construction arctique vivante et pleine de ressources, le Kuujjuaq Hackathon, un événement de conception-construction de cinq jours, a démontré à quel point des ressources limitées peuvent être une inspiration pour la conception et comment les communautés peuvent réintégrer le «social» dans l'espace social.

'Blueprint for a Hack' documente l'événement, en soulignant les éléments critiques d'une méthodologie de piratage réussie pouvant éclairer les pratiques de planification et de conception futures. Bien que centrée sur la réaction des communautés nordiques isolées aux pratiques conventionnelles, ses méthodes ont des implications profondes qui commencent à répondre aux préoccupations globales liées à la conception et aux modes de consommation matérielle, ainsi qu'à la nécessité croissante de faire progresser les approches novatrices en matière de planification et de conception urbaine.

Katerina swings! A swing set stabilized by two palettes. *Cape Christian, NU*. September, 2016.

Wind shelter, a self-built structure made of found lumber and plywood. *Kuujjuarapik, QC*, 2016.

Plywood windscreen designed to minimize snow drifting. *Cape Christian, NU*, 2014.

Self-built workshop with access to front door of a government sponsored house. *Kuujjuaq, QC*, 2016.

Extra storage on ski treads. *Cape Christian, NU*, 2014.

Drying rack in kitchen – made from found lumber and repurposed mosquito screen. *Kuujjuaq, QC*, 2017.

HACKING TRASH
PIRATAGE

The word "hack" invokes a variety of subtly different meanings. Traditionally, these included: to cut, notch, break up, clear, reduce or cope. More contemporary connotations refer to clever but unauthorized system modifications aiming for an outcome other than the original objective. This nuance is reflected more broadly in the Hindi or Punjabi word 'jugaad' meaning a flexible approach to problem-solving using limited resources. For Inuit, the notion emphasizes a do-it-yourself tip, trick or method for improvising simple, frugal solutions. This notion of hacking is embedded in the rich informal building culture used by Inuit throughout northern Canada.

Le mot "bidouille" évoque une variété de significations subtiles. Celles-ci comprenaient traditionnellement: couper, entailler, casser, nettoyer, réduire ou faire face. Des connotations plus contemporaines font référence à des modifications de système intelligentes mais non autorisées visant un résultat autre que l'objectif initial. Cette nuance est reflétée plus largement dans le mot hindi ou punjabi «jugaad» qui signifie une approche flexible de la résolution de problèmes utilisant des ressources limitées. Pour les Inuits, la notion met l'accent sur un conseil, une astuce ou une méthode à faire soi-même pour improviser des solutions simples et économe. Cette notion de piratage est enracinée dans la riche culture de construction informelle du nord du Canada.

MATERIALS

SPACE

PEOPLE

Available Resources: material + spatial + human resource alliance.

Kuujjuaq's outdoor sports fields in August. *Kuujjuaq, QC*, 2017.

THE KUUJJUAQ HACKATHON
LE HACKATHON DE KUUJJUAQ

The Kuujjuaq Hackathon brought together more than 60 town residents with an interdisciplinary design team from southern Quebec. Organized by McGill University's Minimum Cost Housing / Hackathon Group and the Village of Kuujjuaq, the hack creatively repurposed materials from the village dump to revitalize key public spaces. Over five days in September, 2017, we designed and built an outdoor community structure, to improve recreational opportunities and enhance the village's public realm. Three interconnected challenges, identified by local residents, were the project's driving objectives. (1) Improve the public realm, (2) Reduce landfill waste and (3) Provide cultural exchange opportunities.

Le hackathon de Kuujjuaq a rassemblé plus de 60 résidents de la ville et une équipe de conception interdisciplinaire du sud du Québec. Organisé par le groupe 'Minimum Cost Housing' de l'Université McGill et le village de Kuujjuaq, ce piratage a permis de transformer de façon créative des matériaux provenant de la décharge du village pour revitaliser des espaces publics clés. En septembre 2017, pendant cinq jours, nous avons conçu et construit une structure communautaire en plein air, afin d'améliorer les possibilités de loisirs et de mettre en valeur le domaine public du village. Trois objectifs interdépendants identifiés par les résidents locaux dominaient le projet. (1) Améliorer le domaine public, (2) Réduire les déchets d'enfouissement et (3) Offrir des possibilités d'échange culturel.

Panorama from the Kuujjuaq dump. *Kuujjuaq, QC, 2017.*

Collage created to promote the 2017 Kuujjuaq Hackathon.

Eastward view of the project site. *Kuujjuaq, QC*, 2017.

OBJECTIVE 1. IMPROVE THE PUBLIC REALM
AMÉLIORER LE DOMAINE PUBLIC

Canada's architectural community has paid scant attention to northern communities' public realm. Public structures tend to be virtual copies of southern models and do not address specific northern needs. One example that stood out for the project team was the Kuujjuaq outdoor ice hockey rink. Centrally located beside an expansive field, the area is subject to biting winter winds. Yet no shelter existed for patrons to lace up skates and store boots. Instead, residents drove to the rink and changed inside their vehicles. For those without access to a vehicle, the rink remained largely unused. In the summer, baseball players face similar storage problems, and are left without a place to store valuables when they play.

Les architectes canadiens n'ont guère prêté attention au domaine public des collectivités du Nord. Toutes les structures publiques existantes tendent à être des copies virtuelles des modèles du Sud et ne répondent pas aux besoins spécifiques du Nord. L'équipe de projet s'est notamment distinguée avec la patinoire de hockey en plein air de Kuujjuaq (b). Située au centre d'un vaste terrain, la région est soumise aux vents violents de l'hiver. Pourtant, il n'existait aucun abri pour les clients qui voulaient lacer leurs patins et ranger leurs bottes. Au lieu de cela, les résidents se rendaient à la patinoire et se changeaient dans leur véhicule. Pour ceux qui n'avaient pas accès à un véhicule, la patinoire est restée en grande partie inutilisée. En été, les joueurs de baseball étaient confrontés aux mêmes problèmes de stockage.

Assessing the next steps at the Kuujjuaq dump. *Kuujjuaq, QC*, 2017.

OBJECTIVE 2. REDUCE LANDFILL WASTE
RÉDUIRE LES DÉCHETS D'ENFOUISSEMENT

The predominant approach to managing garbage in Nunavik – the northernmost territory of Quebec – consists of controlled burning, which remains problematic as it contributes to air pollution and atmospheric greenhouse gasses. This project capitalizes on the strong Do-It-Yourself (DIY) building culture that exists in northern communities of Canada, showcasing its relevance as a design approach that can recover, reduce, and recycle waste materials and help rethink our consumption patterns. Dealing with waste in isolated locations also opens broader and more profound questions about contemporary global practices of dealing with waste. How long can our global collection, and waste management value chains continue to expand without causing irreparable harm to the planet's environmental systems? Dealing with waste is becoming an ever more global phenomena, therefore solutions need to emerge that address waste materials on site, and reimagine our packaging and consumption patterns from the ground up.

Au Nunavik, l'approche prédominante de la gestion des ordures – le territoire le plus septentrional du Québec – consiste à brûler de façon contrôlée, ce qui demeure problématique car il contribue à la pollution de l'air et aux gaz à effet de serre atmosphériques.. Ce projet a tiré parti de la forte culture de construction de bricolage prévalant dans le nord du Canada et a démontré sa pertinence en tant qu'approche de conception permettant de récupérer, de réduire et de recycler les déchets et d'aider à repenser nos modes de consommation. La gestion des déchets dans des lieux isolés concentre également l'esprit sur les pratiques mondiales, y compris les différentes chaînes de valeur de collecte, de tri et de recyclage créées pour traiter les déchets qui continuent à se développer dans le monde entier. Le traitement des déchets devient un phénomène de plus en plus global, c'est pourquoi des solutions doivent émerger qui traitent des déchets sur site et réinventer nos modèles d'emballage et de consommation à partir de zéro.

Filling jumbo tires with sand, to be used as foundations for the skating shelter. *Kuujjuaq, QC*, 2017.

OBJECTIVE 3. PROVIDE OPPORTUNITIES FOR DESIGN EXCHANGES BETWEEN SOUTHERN AND NORTHERN GROUPS IN CANADA *OFFRIR DES POSSIBILITÉS D'ÉCHANGES DE CONCEPTION ENTRE LE SUD ET LE NORD DU CANADA*

The very different worlds of northern and southern Canadians rarely interact. With respect to the built environment, government sponsored housing and community plans continue to emerge from mainstream Canadian values and stand as a physical mark of southern values. Unfortunately, there remain few avenues from which conversations about the built environment can occur between groups. This project provides a unique platform in which both groups collaboratively use design to open important conversations about the built environment in northern communities. The final built intervention stands as an example of this DIY approach and demonstrates that design can open conversations about the public realm in northern communities.

Les mondes très différents des Canadiens du nord et du sud interagissent rarement. En ce qui concerne l'environnement bâti, les projets de logement et les projets communautaires parrainés par le gouvernement continuent de se dégager des valeurs canadiennes dominantes du Sud. Malheureusement, il ne reste que peu de possibilités de discussions entre groupes sur l'environnement bâti. Ce projet fournit une plateforme unique dans laquelle les deux groupes utilisent en collaboration la conception pour ouvrir des discussions importantes sur l'environnement bâti dans les communautés du Nord. La dernière intervention est un exemple concret de cette approche de bricolage et démontre que le design peut ouvrir des discussions sur le domaine public des communautés du Nord. L'intervention finale construite est un exemple concret de cette approche de bricolage et démontre que sa conception peut ouvrir des discussions sur le domaine public des communautés du Nord.

Self-built workshop and storage shed. *Inukjuak, QC*. 2017.

The book is organized in three chapters. Chapter One, REMOTE RESOURCEFULNESS, examines how waste is used and managed in remote northern communities. Our investigation begins at the municipal dump, or as locals call it, "the Canadian Tire" (Jacobs et al. 2009). Chapter Two, IN-BETWEEN SPACE, focuses on mining waste and exploring how it can be used as a catalyst to improve public spaces. Chapter Three, HACKING TRASH / THE KUUJJUAQ HACKATHON, considers the practical implications of applying design solutions to problems of waste management. Who decides what we throw away? And what we keep? The chapter chronicles the events of the 2017 Kuujjuaq Hackathon, detailing a successful example of how repurposed waste can be used to reconfigure public space and build stronger communities. The book closes with an Afterword, in which Tunu Napartuk, the former mayor of Kuujjuaq, reflects on the legacy of the event, the current approaches to planning in the North and where to go from here.

Le premier chapitre de cet ouvrage, 'Remote Resourcefulness', examine comment les Inuits gèrent et réutilisent les déchets. Notre enquête commence au dépotoir municipal o, comme l'appellent les locaux, « le magasin Canadian Tire ». Le chapitre deux, In-between Spaces, développe ce thème et son lien avec l'amélioration de l'espace public. Donner forme à des espaces quotidiens au moyen de piratages simples et inventifs peut transformer la façon dont les gens interagissent avec leur environnement et construire des communautés plus fortes. Nous croyons que les hacks créent une place pour l'engagement de la communauté. Le chapitre trois, 2017 Kuujjuaq Hackathon, illustre les implications pratiques de l'application de solutions de conception aux problèmes de gestion des déchets. Enfin, le maire Tunu, l'ancien maire de Kuujjuaq, revient sur l'héritage de l'évènement et soulève des points importants sur les approches actuelles en matière de planification dans le Nord et la voie à suivre.

Peter Jacobs, Daniel Berrouard and Paul Mireille. "Nunavik: A homeland in transition." *Kuujjuaq, Kativik Environmental Quality Commission*. http://www. keqc-cqek. ca/KEQC- AR09-eF-lo. pdf (2009).

REMOTE RESOURCEFULNESS

A three bedroom, off-grid house, built from found materials including a shipping container. *Clyde River, NU*, 2015.

DUPONT
Tyvek
HomeWrap
Call 1-800-44TYVEK WWW.TYVEK.COM
DUPONT The miracles of science

Ice formations outside Cape Christian. *Cape Christian, NU*, 2015.

THE CANADIAN NORTH: A CONTEXTUAL OVERVIEW

Canada's North, a part of the Arctic circumpolar region, is homeland to about 43,000 Inuit. Meaning "the people" in the Inuktitut language, Inuit and their ancestors have occupied Nunangat, "where Inuit live," for millennia. There are four Inuit regions: Nunatsiavut along Labrador's northern coast, Nunavik in northern Quebec, the territory of Nunavut, and the Inuvialuit region in the Northwest Territories. For its part, the Government of Canada has four priorities for this land and its people: To exercise sovereignty, protect its environmental heritage, promote its social and economic development, and improve and devolve Northern governance.

NORTHERN SETTLEMENTS

LIST OF SETTLEMENTS

Aklavik
Akulivik – AKU
Alert
Arctic Bay – ARB
Arviat – ARV
Aupaluk – AUP
Baker Lake – BAK
Bathurst Inlet
Bécancour - BEC
Cambridge Bay – CAM
Cape Dorset – DOR
Chesterfield Inlet – CHE
Churchill – CHU
Clyde River – CLY
Contrecoeur - CON
Coral Harbour – COR
Eureka – EUR
Gjoa Haven – GJO
Grande-Anse - GRA
Grise Fiord – GRI
Hall Beach – HAL
Happy Valley-Goose Bay
Igloolik – IGL
Inukjuaq
Iqaluit – IQA
Ivujivik – IVU
Kangiqsujuaq – KAQ
Kangiqsualujjuaq – KAL
Kangirsuk – KAN
Kimmirut – KIM
Kugaaruk – KGA
Kugluktuk – KGL
Kuujjuaq – KUU
Kujjuarapik
Matane - MAT
Milne Inlet – MIL
Montreal – MTL
Nain – NAI
Nanisivik – NAN
Nuuk – GOH
Pangnirtung – PAN
Pond Inlet – PON
Puvirnituq – PUV
Quaqtaq – QUA
Quebec – QUE
Qikiqtarjuaq – QKQ
Rankin Inlet – RAN
Naujaat - NAU
Resolute Bay – RES
Salluit – SAL
Sanikiluaq – SAN
Sept-Iles – SIL
Taloyoak – TAL
Tasiujaq – TAS
Thule – THU
Trois Rivieres
Ulukhaktok (Holman Island)
Umiujaq – UMI
Valleyfield – VAL

400km

A VAST LAND

Almost four million square kilometres, Inuit Nunangat consists of 40 percent of Canada's land mass. Very few communities are connected via roads to southern Canada, with access confined to air and sea routes. Most northern villages have an airport and many are situated on major waterways allowing up to three shipments of goods via sealift each year. In winter, ice roads link some communities to the South.

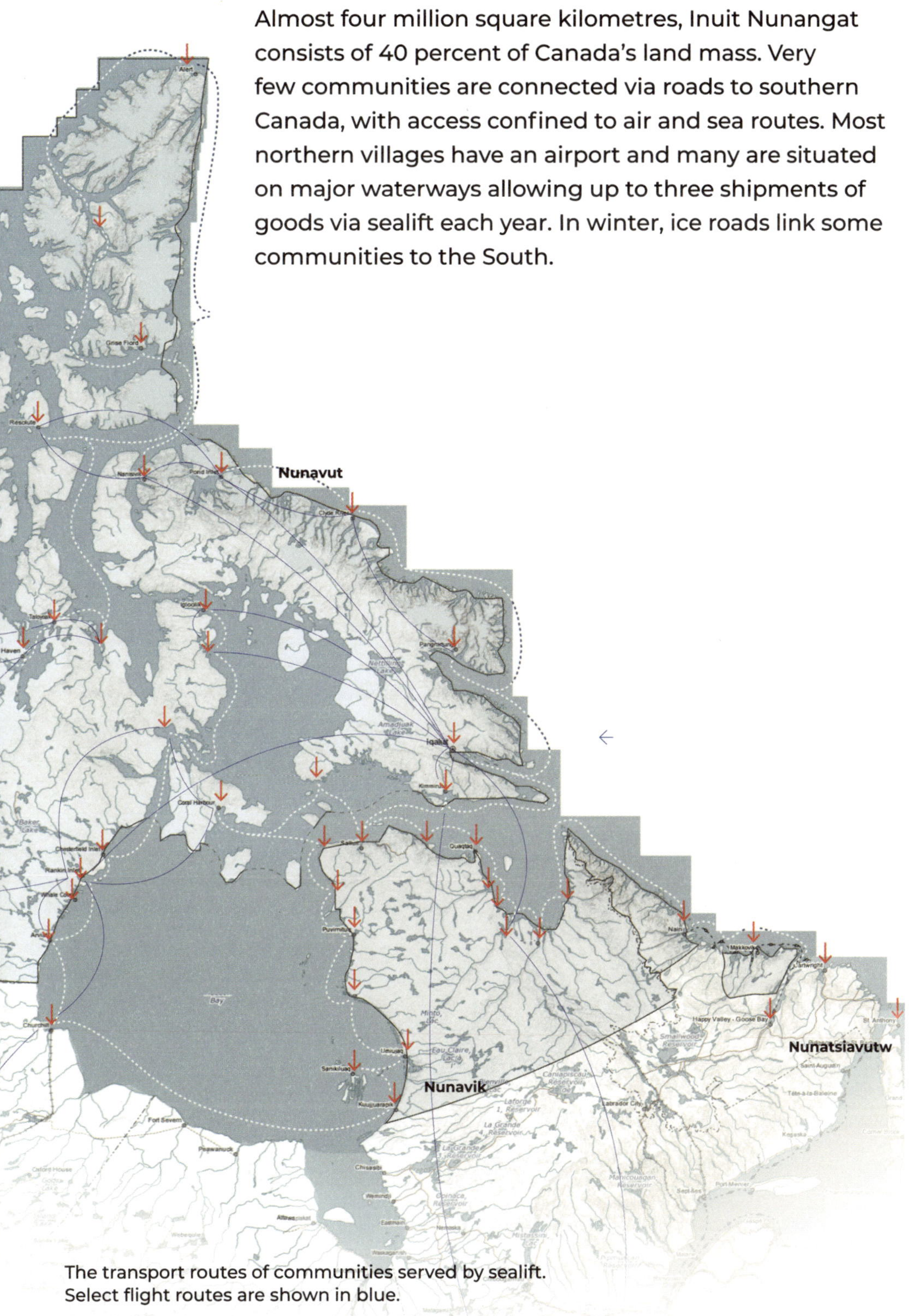

The transport routes of communities served by sealift. Select flight routes are shown in blue.

Fall colors. *Kuujjuaq, QC* 2017,

NUNAVIK AND KUUJJUAQ

Comprising the northern third of the province of Quebec, Nunavik, meaning “the Great Land” in Inuktitut, is about as big as Spain. Some 12,000 people, 90 percent Inuit, call Nunavik home.

Bisected by the tree line, which marks the edge between tundra and boreal forest, Nunavik features both Arctic and subarctic climates. During long, severe winters, temperatures drop to an average of -24C°. Brief summers seldom see temperatures above +15C°. Nunavik's range of latitudes implies short winter-time days that lengthen in summer.

Nine of its 14 villages are situated on tundra and, apart from its southernmost town, all are built on permafrost. With rising temperatures, this thick subsurface of normally frozen soil is melting, destabilizing existing structures and threatening current approaches to building in the region. A changing climate is also disrupting local fauna and flora, directly influencing traditional hunting, fishing and food gathering and intensifying dependence on external food sources.

Set near Ungava Bay's southern shore, Kuujjuaq is the region's largest village and its administrative capital. No roadways connect it or any of the thirteen remaining villages to southern Quebec. Instead, residents rely on expensive daily air traffic or seasonal sealift to transport goods, people, and their waste. The community's isolation limits the transfer of municipal garbage to regional waste management or recycling centres, which has led to a range of environmental problems.

MATERIAL ACCESS

There are two predominant methods in which goods make their way to northern remote communities.

Wood crates used to transport goods via sealift. *Clyde River, NU,* 2015.

SEALIFT

Materials, loaded into crates or sea canisters in southern Quebec, reach remote northern communities over the course of several months. Typical cargo includes, vehicles, building construction materials and nonperishable food.

Luggage stored in an Air Inuit de Havilland Twin Otter airplane. *Kuujjuaq, QC,* 2017.

AIR CARGO

Most communities see regular air traffic on a daily basis. Airplanes will typically portion off a section of the plane for cargo. Typical air cargo includes, perishable foods, medical supplies and mail.

ATVs (Hondas)
cars / trucks
snowmobiles
canoes
non-perishables
engines
construction materials
seasonal clothing
hunting equipment
electronics
municipal equipment
heavy machinery
automotive equipment
rifles
household appliances
stationary
landscaping materials
wood
vehicles
tires
barrels
septic tanks
water tanks
paints
tools
batteries
generators
glass containers
plastics
textiles

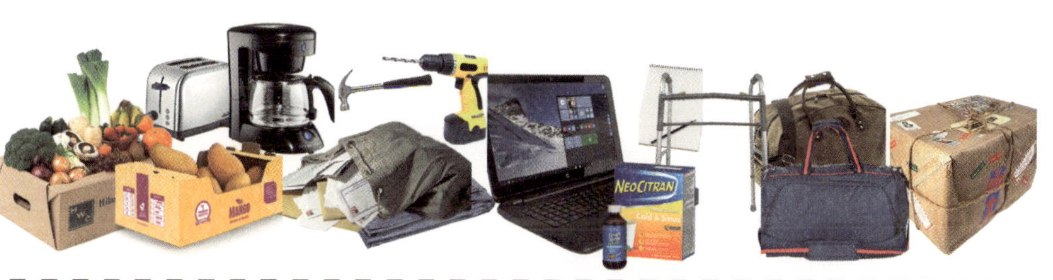

mail items
perishable fresh foods
medical supplies
medical equipment
general store goods
construction tools
text books
electronics
clothing
parcels
luggage
small household
appliances
craft supplies
textiles
dental supplies
stationary
photographic
equipment

Diagram depicting typical items transported via sea lift and air cargo.

WASTE IN NUMBERS

The Kativik Regional Government estimates that the average resident of Nunavik produces almost 10 cubic meters of waste per year. This is slightly more than southern Canadians. The entire regions of Nunavik will therefore produce 12,000 tonnes of waste each year, or equivalent of 8,716 garbage truck loads. In Kuujjuaq, a village with a population of just over 2,000, this amounts to 22,893 m3, enough to fill 1,635 garbage trucks (KRG, 2016).

With some of Canada's fastest growing populations, northern communities must rethink waste management patterns.

Garbage Truck holds 14 cubic meters of waste.

Renewable Resources, Environment, Lands and Parks, et al. "Nunavik Residual Materials Management Plan." *Nunavik Residual Materials Management Plan*, *2015*. www.krg.ca/ images/stories/docs/Environment/ PGMR_Eng.pdf.

Population growth in Nunavik. The region's total population is expected to grow at a rate of 16.6 % between 2006 and 2031, totaling 12,770 persons.

Nunavik's total annual volume of trash represented in dump truck loads.

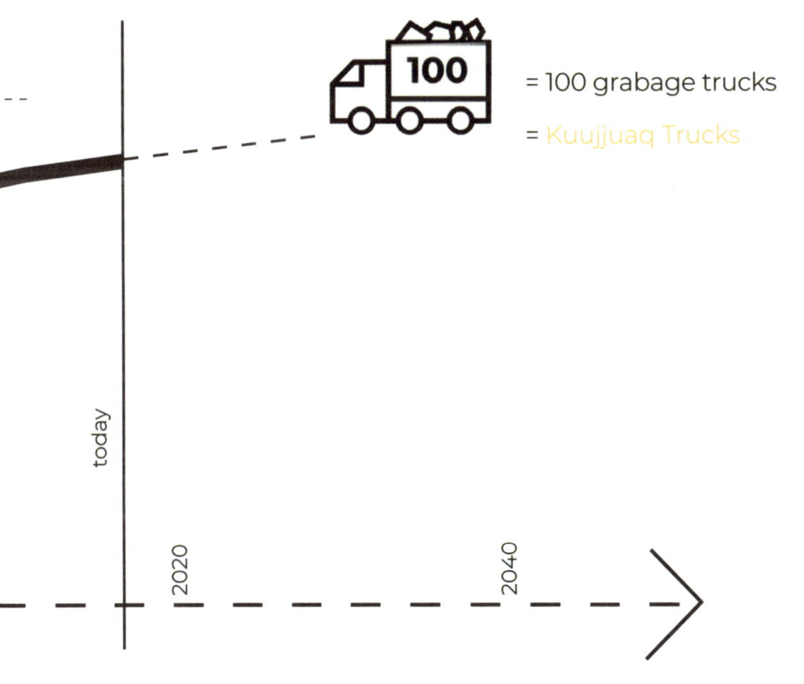

WASTE IN NUNAVIK

Municipal waste makes up 56 percent of the region's total landfill waste. The Construction, Renovation and Demolition sector accounts for about 35 percent. Industrial, Commercial or Institutional activities produce the remainder (see pie chart on page 47).

The pie chart's outer circle provides a breakdown of the types of waste generated in Nunavik. Items listed in blue indicate legacy waste, that which is not further processed by either burning or landfilling.

A sampling of typical waste materials.

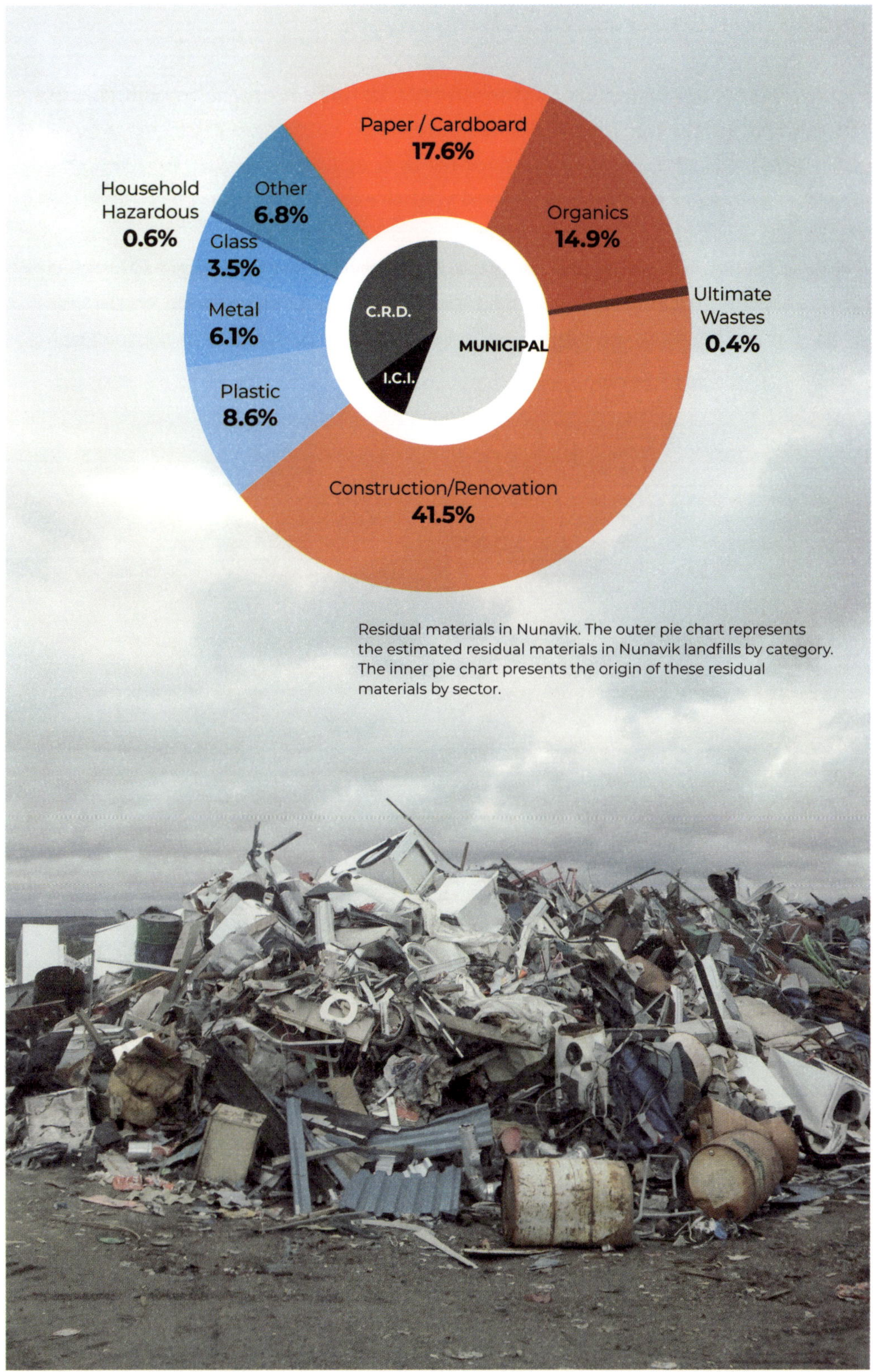

Residual materials in Nunavik. The outer pie chart represents the estimated residual materials in Nunavik landfills by category. The inner pie chart presents the origin of these residual materials by sector.

Household appliances piled at the dump. *Kuujjuaq, QC*, 2017.

THE NORTHERN VILLAGE DUMP

All northern villages organize their dump. Usually found a few kilometers outside the settlement, dump sites receive all kinds of waste and are equipped with heavy machinery for landfill operations. Very few restrict access, so anyone can deposit – and withdraw – trash on their own.

Waste is sorted. Large reusable items, for instance, are stored in designated areas. A few communities separate recyclables for shipment south for processing. Anything left over is either destined for landfill or burned in open air.

Materials organized for reuse at the Kuujjuaq Dump. *Kuujjuaq, QC*, 2017.

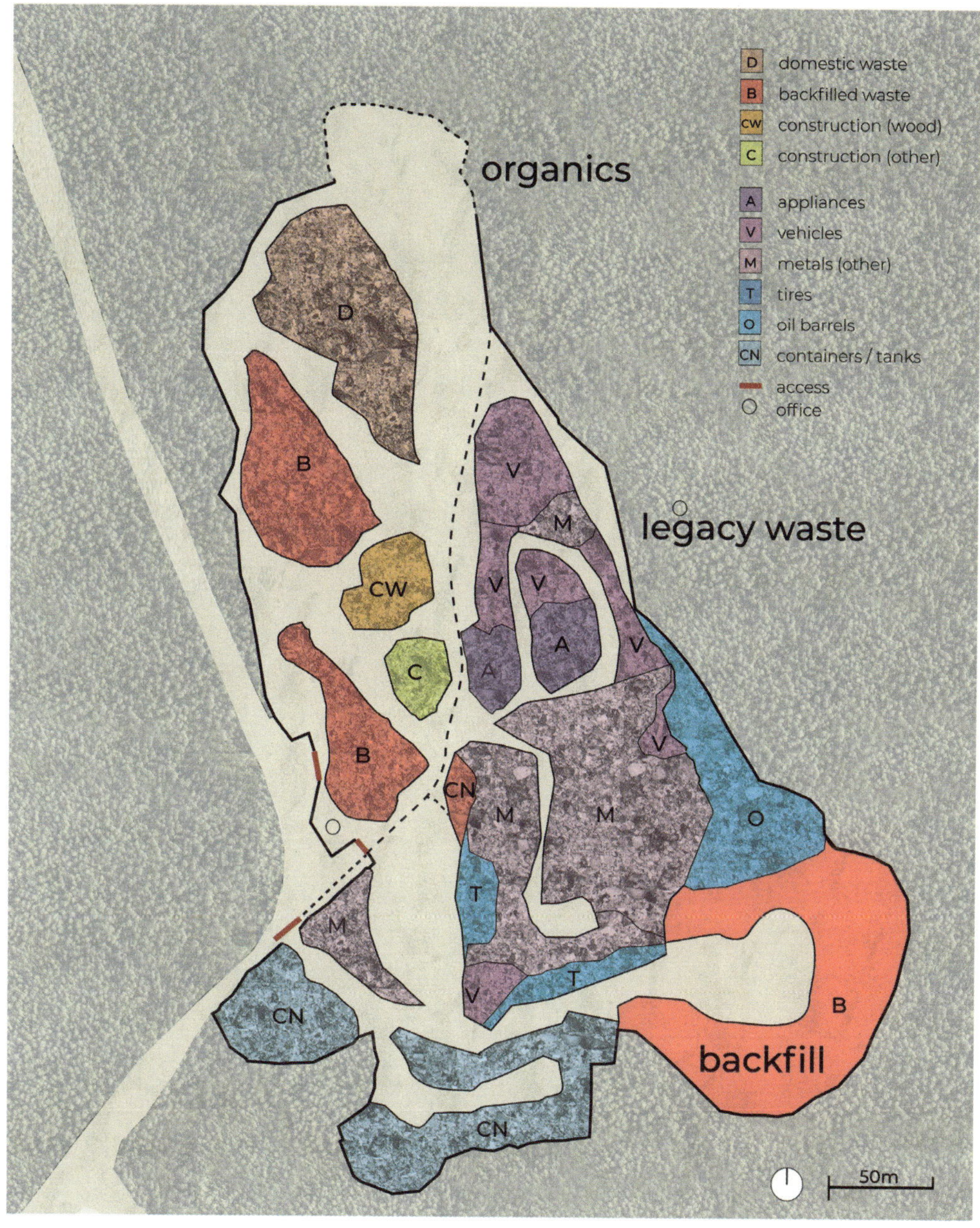

Kuujjuaq dump operations. Diagram depicting the size and distribution of waste in the village dump.

Bicycle section at the dump. *Kuujjuaq, QC*, 2017.

Legacy waste. *Kuujjuaq, QC*, 2017.

HACKING MATERIAL

Municipal “legacy” waste refers to things like end-of-life vehicles, drums, white goods, used tires and other sorts of materials that can accumulate in and around communities over decades. At the Kuujjuaq dump, scrap vehicles (bicycles, cars, trucks, snowmobiles, ATVs, motorcycles, boats and heavy equipment) are sorted into their own section. While select government sponsored recycling programs exist for specific items such as oil drums or tires, the transport costs of shipping recyclables to operation centres in southern Quebec is prohibitive, and a centralized large-scale recycling program does not yet exist. Smaller, community-led solutions may be the answer.

A GROWING PROBLEM

With no way to permanently dispose of select legacy and other waste, the Kuujjuaq Landfill is quickly expanding.

2004

2% growth / year

2012

8% growth / year

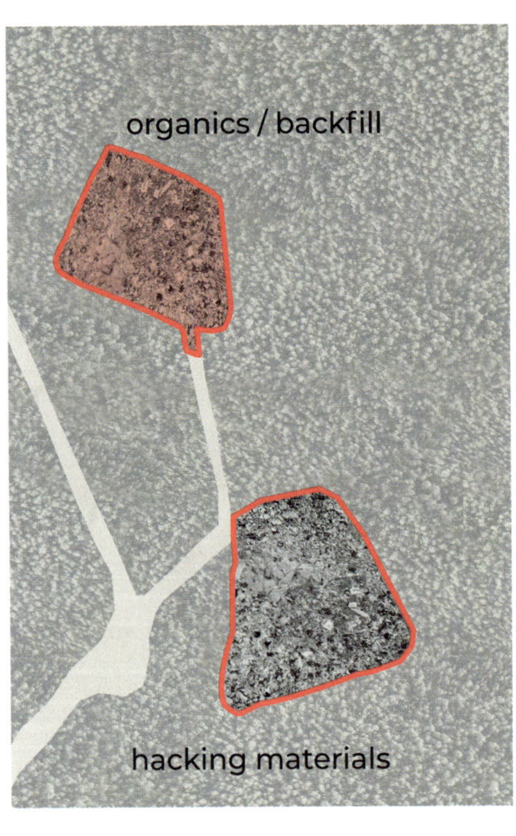

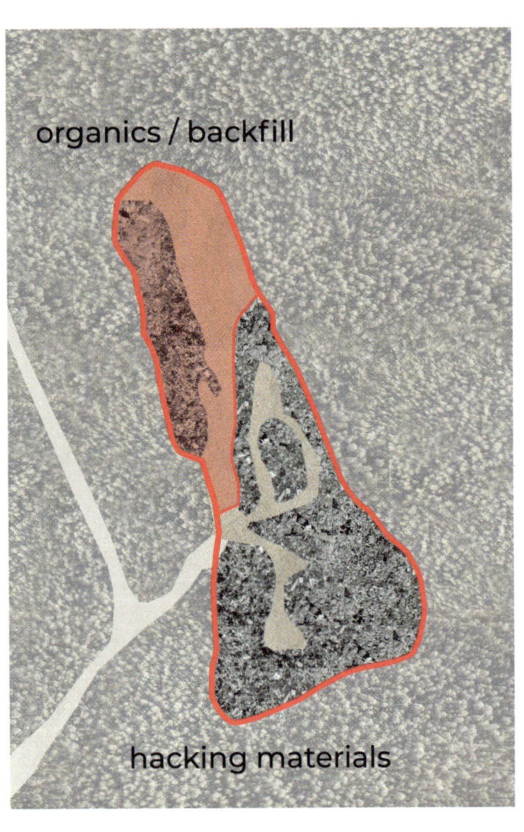

	2004
Organics / Backfill	13,677 m2
Hacking Materials	18,167 m2
	31,844 m2

	2012
Organics / Backfill	14,877 m2
Hacking Materials	34,699 m2
	49,576 m2

Kuujjuaq dump operations. A study of aerial photos taken in 2004, 2012 and 2017.

2017

13% growth / year

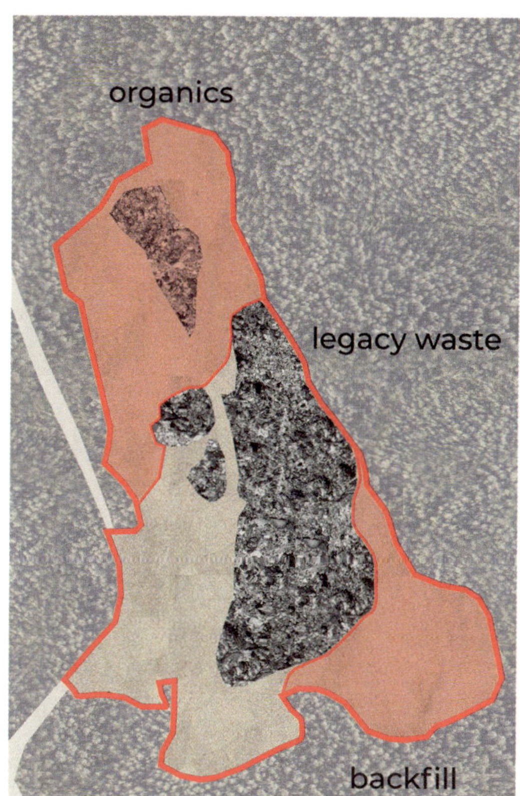

Organics / Backfill	38,781 m2
Hacking Materials	52,353 m2
	91,134 m2

The Kuujjuaq Dump in 2018 (red outline), overlaid atop a map of the Village of Kuujjuaq. In 2018 the dump consumes a total of 91,134m2.

Based on the village's current growth rates, the expected size of the Kuujjuaq dump in 2040 will be 260,664m2.

Kuujjuaq dump operations. Landfilling and burning (right), legacy waste storage (foreground left). *Kuujjuaq, QC, 2017*

"If it can't be reduced, reused, repaired, rebuilt, refurbished, refinished, resold, recycled, or composted then it should be restricted, redesigned or removed from production."

- Pete Seeger *If It Can't Be Reduced*, 2008

THE OFFICIAL RECYCLING PROGRAMS

A few communities separate recyclables for shipment to southern Quebec for processing. Items include tires, oil drums and plastic bottles. These programs have proven inefficient and costly.

Mounds of tires waiting to be shipped to southern Quebec where they can be recycled. *Kuujjuaq, QC*, 2017.

Crushed oil drums, re-packed inside a sealift container, for shipping to southern Quebec. *Kuujjuaq, QC, 2017.*

IN-BETWEEN SPACE

The "In-between". Cabins, containers and materials for future construction projects surround government housing. *Kuujjuaq, QC, 2017.*

Snowmobile tracks are repurposed to provide a skidproof path to an outdoor workshop. *Kuujjuaq, QC*, 2017.

Outdoor workshop. *Inukjuak, QC*, 2017.

PUBLIC SPACE: CONTEMPORARY INUIT IDENTITY AND THE "IN-BETWEEN"

As in the South, outdoor space is social space and the most vibrant communal spaces in northern communities are found around and in-between houses. Here, undifferentiated plots, uniformly blanketed by sand or gravel, serve as an essential extension to the house, a place to gather, work or just to smoke.

While boundaries are fluid, each house's plot is defined by the objects scattered on the ground. Most of those objects end up as architectural components – outbuildings and mobile cabins (Havelka, 2018). Planners and architects are only recently discovering the "in-betweens" creative energy and potential.

Havelka, Susane. *Building with IQ (Inuit Qaujimajatuqangit): The rise of a hybrid design tradition in Canada's Eastern Arctic.* Diss. McGill University, 2018.

Informal Roads. "In-between" spaces are used as roadways to the village's central open space. *Kuujjuaq, QC*, 2017.

PUBLIC SPACE IN THE REMOTE NORTH

Northern planners have overlooked public spaces, which scholars and architects have studied, as they invoke history, cultural roots and/or identities. The residual spaces in-between planned housing and infrastructure of northern communities, cannot generate feelings of belonging or produce a sense of rootedness if they are forgotten or left over; that may characterize indifference, negligence or placelessness of many northern villages. These in-between places may be generic and mundane but in the case of the North, they are the places of gatherings, games, and often provide important informal paths in a community's circulation network. Can they not also be recognized as impressive in their own right?

While the playing fields, empty lots, and the informal circulation system, may not be aesthetically pleasing to all, they do serve a purpose and with a little effort can achieve a lot more. In the Northern context, these spaces may be the most commonly used public outdoor areas. They are the places where kids and parents interact, people meet or exchange a few words, traveling or walking or cycling. These few places communities share. They may be unremarkable and characterless or left over but their utility and the frequency with which they are used make them deserve a second look. The first task is to uncover their value, their benefit, their purpose and communal interest.

Beyond this specific objective, our intent was to address community needs on this particular piece of land. Additionally, in a simple way, it answers that need at minimum cost.

Kuujjuaq figure ground diagram depicting the *in-between* spaces of central Kuujjuaq.

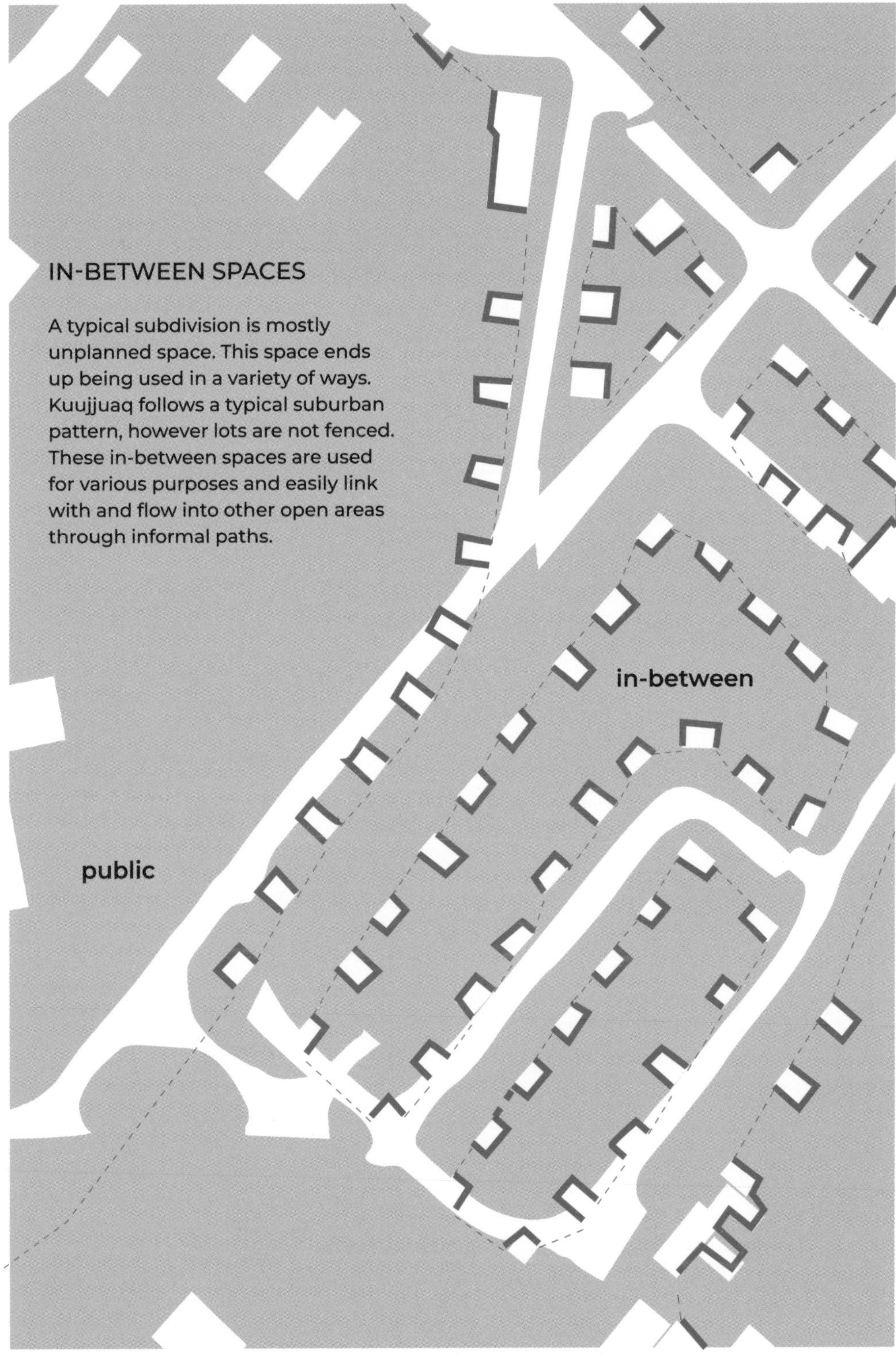

Kuujjuaq figure ground (higher resolution), emphasizing the *in-between* garden spaces behind government housing, and the centrally located public space used as the site of the Hackathon project.

SPACE BETWEEN GOVERNMENT HOUSING

The footprint of a single family government sponsored house consumes 19% of the lot it is designed for and built on. This provides ample "unplanned" space in and around houses, that local residents often use in a variety of ways.

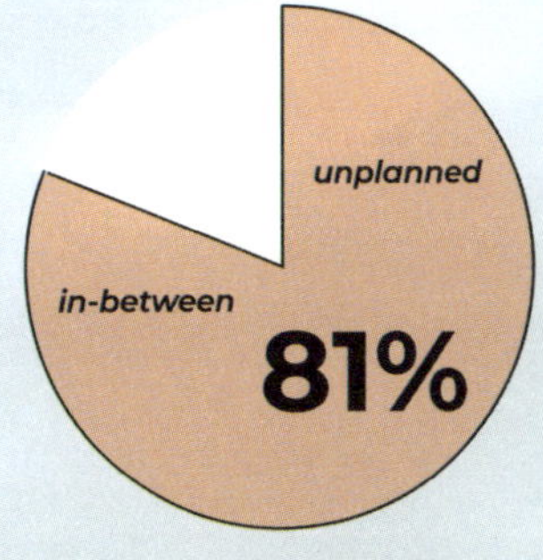

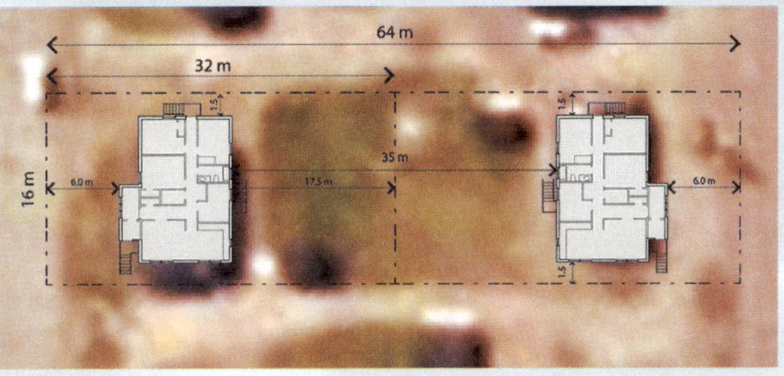

Diagram depicting the average amount of unplanned space associated with new housing developments in Nunavik.

The space behind government housing. Yard space accommodates informal workshops, offices and storage areas. *Kuujjuarapik, QC,* 2017.

Ice rink created in the space between two government houses. *Whapmagoostui, QC*, 2016.

Informal roads and storage established in space between government housing. *Kuujjuarapik, QC*, 2016.

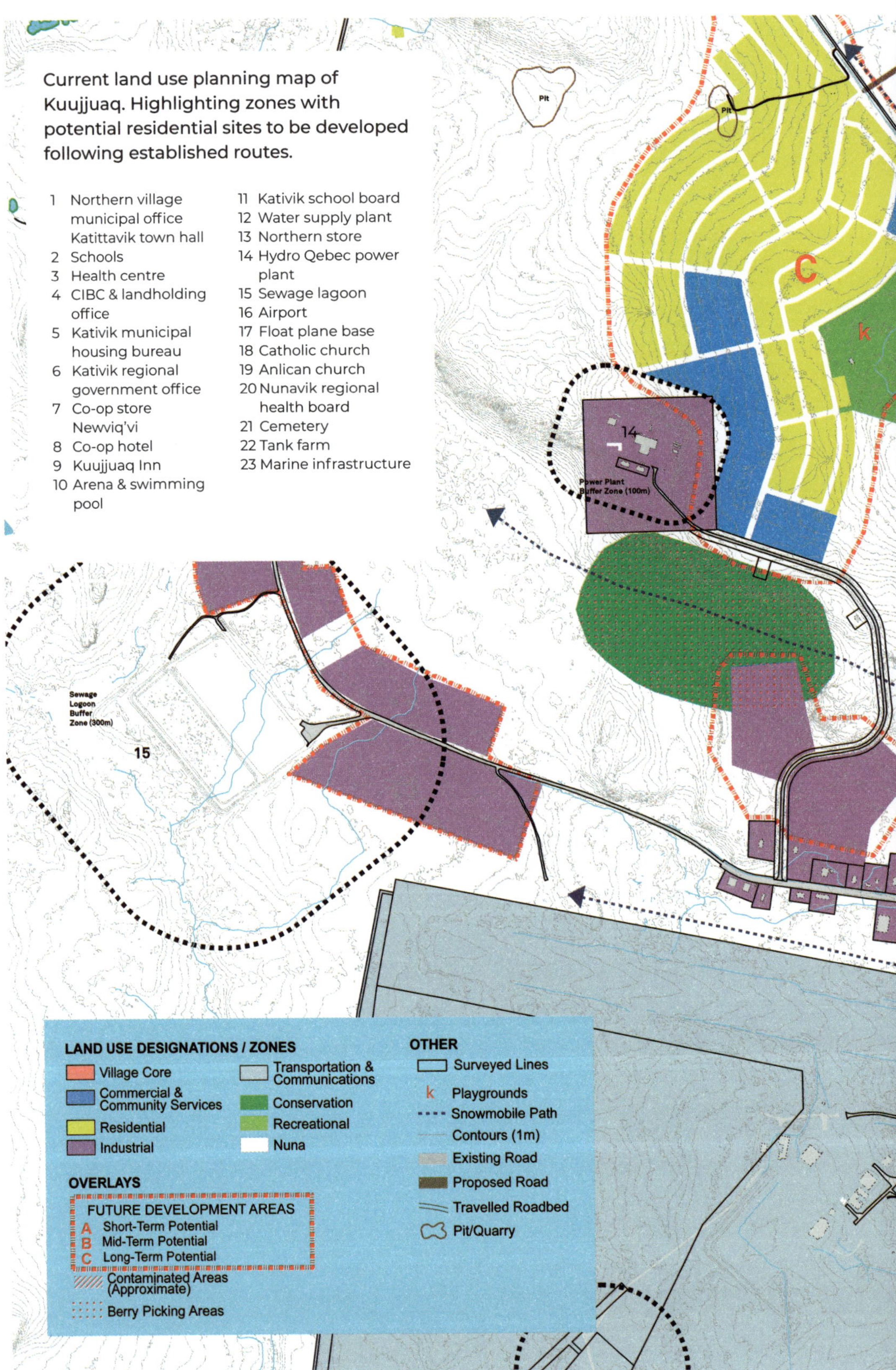

Current land use planning map of Kuujjuaq. Highlighting zones with potential residential sites to be developed following established routes.

1 Northern village municipal office Katittavik town hall
2 Schools
3 Health centre
4 CIBC & landholding office
5 Kativik municipal housing bureau
6 Kativik regional government office
7 Co-op store Newviq'vi
8 Co-op hotel
9 Kuujjuaq Inn
10 Arena & swimming pool
11 Kativik school board
12 Water supply plant
13 Northern store
14 Hydro Qebec power plant
15 Sewage lagoon
16 Airport
17 Float plane base
18 Catholic church
19 Anlican church
20 Nunavik regional health board
21 Cemetery
22 Tank farm
23 Marine infrastructure

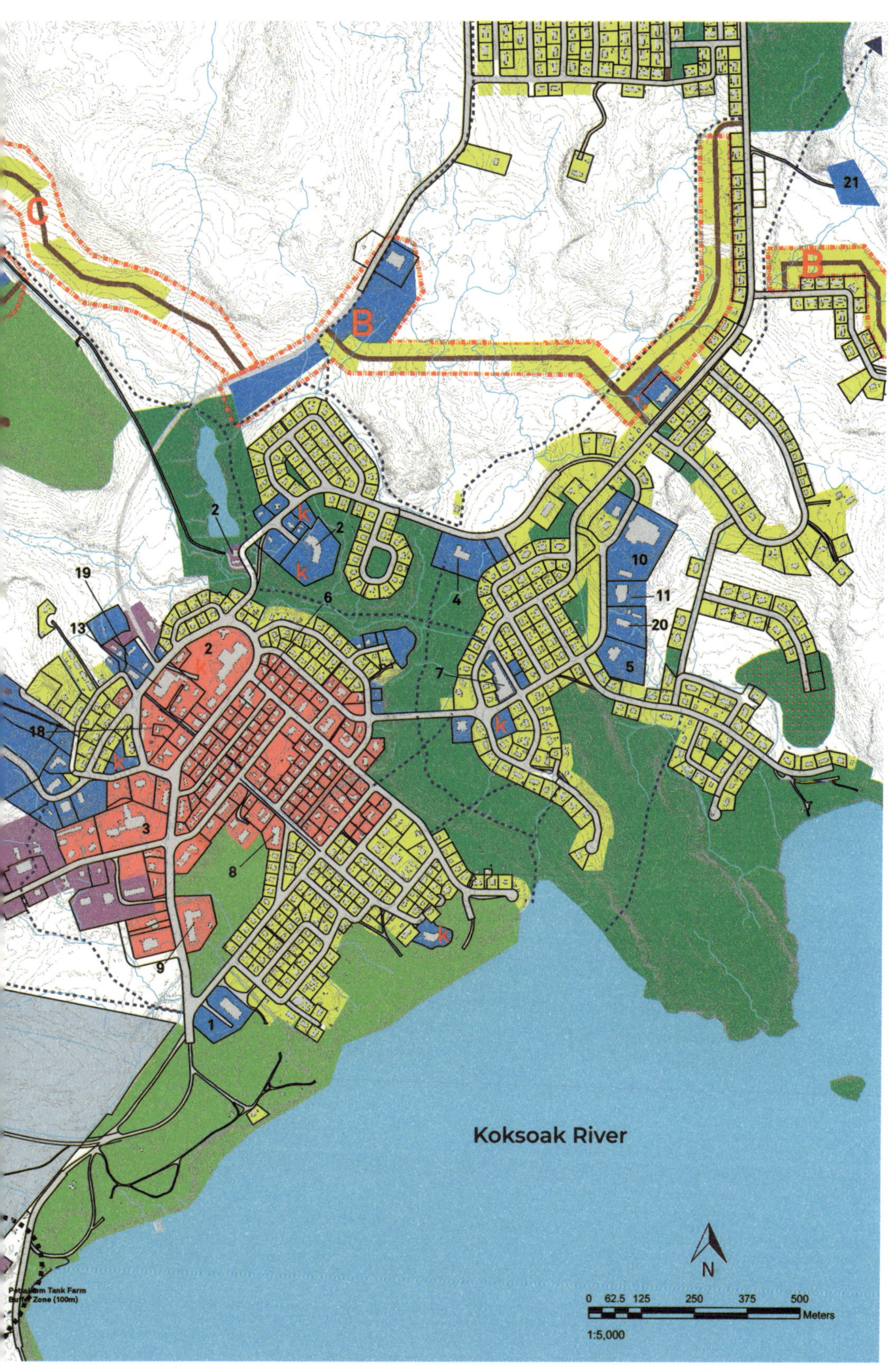
C
B
B
21
2
2
k
k
19
13
6
4
10
11
20
5
7
18
k
2
3
8
9
1
k
Koksoak River
Tank Farm
Zone (100m)
N
0 62.5 125 250 375 500
Meters
1:5,000

ᐃᒻᒥᓂᒃ
ᐊᖅᑭᓱᕆᐊᓂᒃ

Recomposer
le Nord

CCA  Université de Montréal UQÀM   Canadä

Poster for the 2016 Inter-university charrette, hosted by the Canadian Centre for Architecture.

REASSEMBLING THE NORTH

An Opportunity: In 2016, the Canadian Center for Architecture invited Vikram Bhatt to lead the 21st Inter-university charrette co-curated with Susane Havelka and Lisa Koperqualuq. The charrette is an annual event organized by the Canadian Centre for Architecture and McGill University, in collaboration with the Université du Québec à Montréal and the Université de Montréal. Several other universities from across Quebec and Ontario participated, including Concordia University, Université de Laval, Carleton University, Ryerson University, the University of Toronto, the University of Waterloo and Laurentian University. The charrette was open to students and recent graduates in architecture, landscape architecture, environmental design, urban design, planning, industrial design and graphic design. The charrette, entitled Reassembling the North, invited young designers to reconsider Arctic villages, propose simple, cost effective alternatives in Northern settlements and help create livable communities simply and frugally. The theme of Northern communities generated much interest and more than 110 entries were received. Engagement and design qualities were considered “of the highest order”.

The jury members for the charette included, Lola Sheppard (Architect, Professor of Architecture at the University of Waterloo), Mylene Riva, (Professor in Geography at McGill and Canada Chair in Housing, Health and Community), Tunu Napartuk (Mayor of Kuujjuaq), Geneviève Vachon (Professor of Architecture at Université Laval), Rafico Ruiz (Roberta Bondar Postdoctoral Fellow in Northern and Polar Studies at Trent University), Vikram Bhatt (Professor, Director of Minimum Cost Housing Group, McGill University) and Susane Havelka (Architect, PhD, McGill University).

Ecran (2st prize - tie)

Hacking Workshops Ateliers
(3rd prize)

Shared Snowmobile Garages
(1st prize)

Ceci n'est pas un seuil (2nd prize - tie)

A selection of entry panels from the *Reassembling the North* inter-university charrette.
Prize winning entries are titled. Unmarked entries are a random sample of the charrette's 70+ entries.

The jury used three principals to evaluate the submissions. Proposals should:

1. Cleverly make use of available "waste" materials.
2. Aim to be frugal, inclusive and pragmatic, working with available expertise in northern communities.
3. Encourage collaboration among multiple groups and agencies, facilitating conversations about leadership in the design of northern communities.

Mayor Tunu Napartuk, one of the Jury members advocated for this approach: *"We have never been part of the process, they are always imposed. We just accept it but we have our own suggestions"*. With these comments, the idea to reproduce this charrette in a Northern village was born. The charrette would take form as a Hack instead of a charrette as various forms of Hacking are a long-standing tradition in Inuit communities and a part of their culture. It can be seen as either the exploration of transforming found materials in their crafts or the design and implementation of creative inventions such as their cabins and workshops that demonstrate ingenuity and cleverness.

Presenting the 2016 inter-university Charette at the opening ceremony . Charette Curators Vikram Bhatt, Susane Havelka, and Lisa Koperqualuk answer questions from participants.

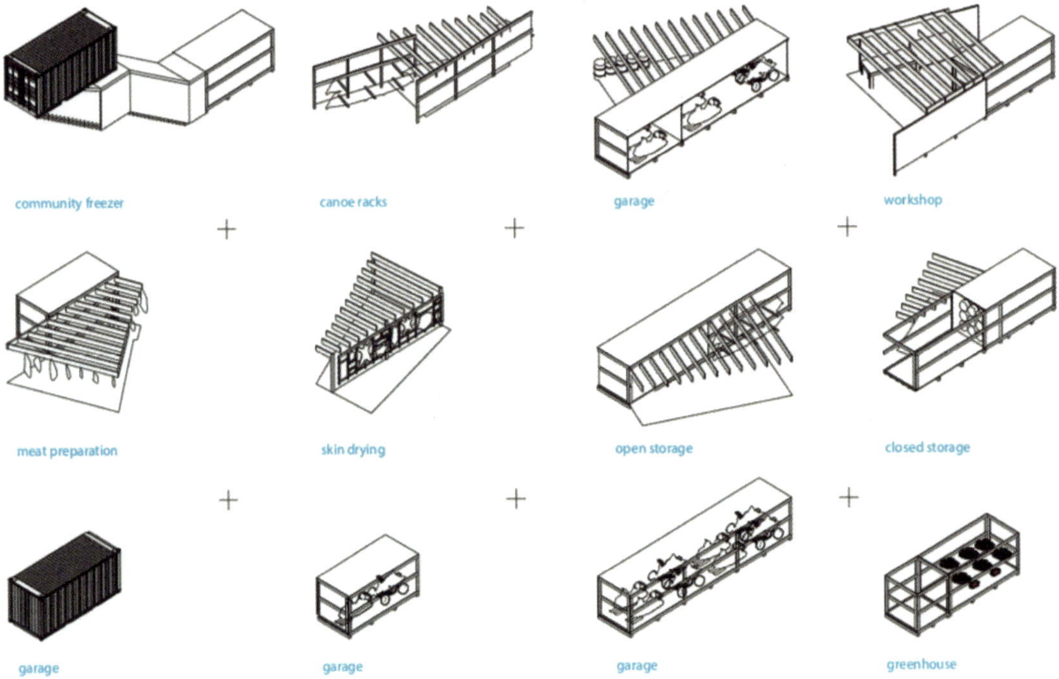

community freezer + canoe racks + garage + workshop

meat preparation + skin drying + open storage + closed storage

garage + garage + garage + greenhouse

Diagram detailing possible configurations of a proposed garage space, taken from the winning charrette entry *"Shared Snowmobile Garages"*.

A gathering place is extremely important to the Inuit. Everyone can take advantage of this space.

Tunu Napartuk, Mayor of Kuujjuaq, 2017.

An image taken from the winning charrette entry *"Shared Snowmobile Garages"*.

SHARED SNOWMOBILE GARAGES
(First place charrette entry)

Tristan Leahy, McGill University
Justin Bouttell, McGill University
Simon McKenzie, McGill University

This proposal introduces a series of decentralized nodes throughout the village. Nodes will address different needs, and can be designed for year-round, multipurpose use.

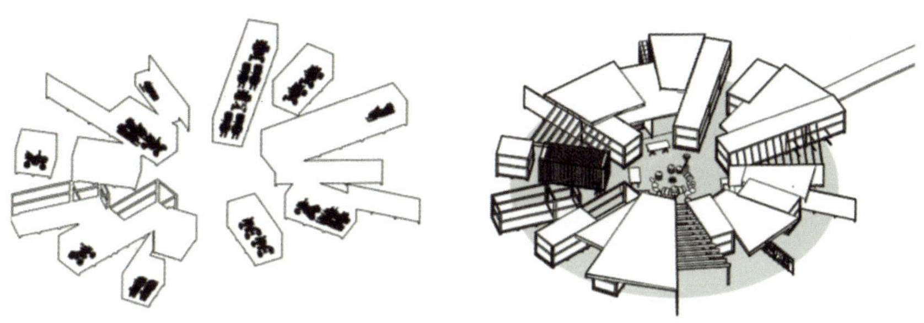

Diagram of garage options from the winning charrette entry *"Shared Snowmobile Garages".*

A second image taken from the winning charrette entry *"Shared Snowmobile Garages".*

An image from the charette entry *"Ecran"*.

ÉCRAN
(Second place-tie charrette entry)

Maxime Hurtubise, Université de Montréal
Andrée-Anne Caron-Boisvert, Université de Montréal
Patrick Pedneault, Université de Montréal

Écran proposes the construction of snow deflectors that are built from plywood and scrap lumber and used to protect houses from harsh weather.

"The concept is simple and realizable."
Tunu Napartuk, Mayor of Kuujjuaq, 2017.

bête,
estin. »

Mayor Tunu Napartuk congratulates the second-place winning entrants from team "Écran". *Montréal, QC,* 2016.

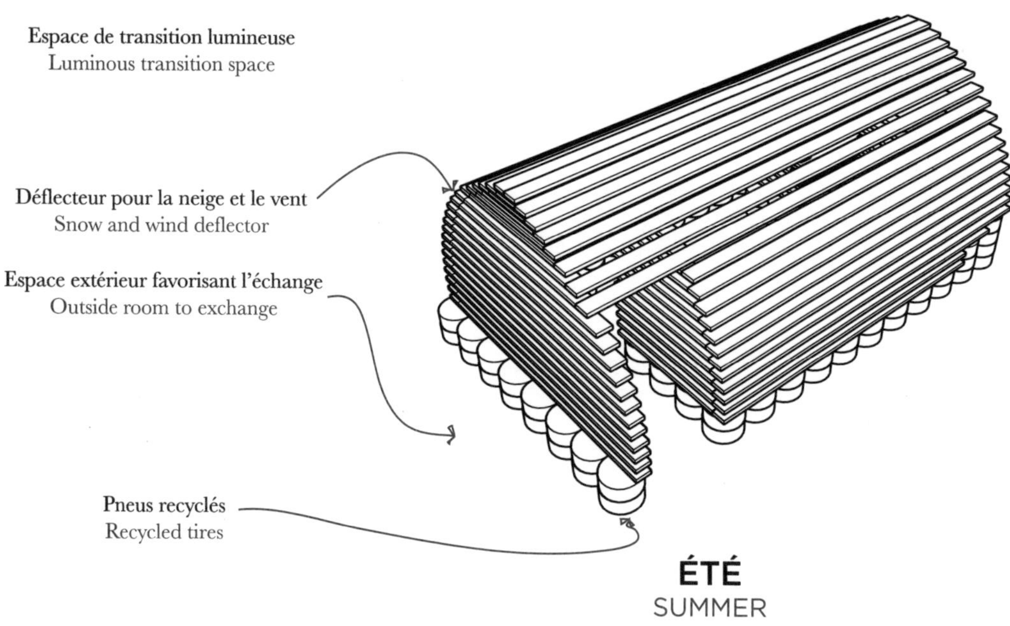

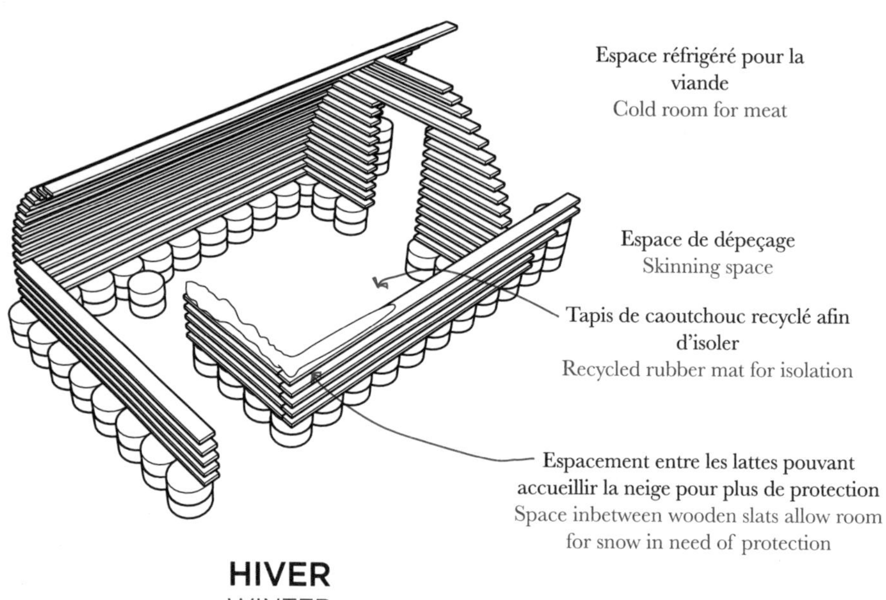

Diagrams from the charette entry "This is Not a Threshold".

THIS IS NOT A THRESHOLD
(Second place-tie charrette entry)

Gabrielle Marquis, Université Laval
Alexandre Morin, Université Laval
Flavie Martineau, Université Laval

The traditional Inuit threshold offers a distinct and smooth transition experience from inside a dwelling to its interior. Inspired by the traditional wisdom used in the igloo entrance, this proposal introduces a new shelter beside a house that is used to ease the transition between inside and outside.

An image from the charette entry titled "This is Not a Threshold".

ᐃᒻᒥᓂᒃ

REASSEMBLING
THE NORTH

ᐊᖅᑭᓱᕆᐊᓚᒃ

RECOMPOSER
LE NORD

ᐃᒻᒥᓂᒃ ᐊᖅᑭᓱᕆᐊᓚᒃ

HACKING WORKSHOPS-ATELIERS

ᓴᓪᓗᐃᑦ

SALLUIT

WHEN - QUAND :
20/21-05-2017

WHERE - OÙ :
gymnasium - gymnase
école pigiurvik school
J0M 1S0, salluit (qc)

20.05 FRIDAY - VENDREDI

AM. DISCUSSIONS
with local stakeholders, craftsmen, experts and ing./arch.
avec les citoyens, artisans, experts et ing./arch

COMMUNITY MEAL - REPAS PARTAGÉ

PM. HACK | BRAINSTORM
in-situ material inventory
tool gathering & hack planning
inventaire des matériaux in situ, collecte d'outils et planification du hack

21.05 SATURDAY - SAMEDI

HACK | BUILDIND SESSION
SESSIONS DE CONSTRUCTION
work groups with the input of craftsmen and experts
groupes de travail assisté d'artisans et d'experts

→

Image from *Hacking Workshops* - Ateliers charette entry.

HACKING WORKSHOPS – ATELIERS

(Third place charrette entry)

Kassandra Bonneville, Université de Montréal
Maggie Cabana, Université de Montréal
Emmanuelle Lauzier, Université de Montréal

Hacking Workshops are a series of community-based events that will take place in the 14 villages of Nunavik. The workshops will provide an opportunity for community members to creatively use waste materials to build objects or spaces that can be used to solve specific northern needs.

"We have to do this! It shows how to organize and structure outside-the-box thinking".

Tunu Napartuk, Mayor of Kuujjuaq, 2017.

Poster created to promote the Hackathon event.

BRINGING THE IDEA TO KUUJJUAQ

The following year, fresh with the design charette's ideas and excitement, the 2017 Kuujjuaq Hackathon brought the concept to the northern community of Kuujjuaq. The team challenges themselves to design a structure using found materials. The intention was twofold: valorize the already well established informal building practices found throughout northern Canada and to engage and empower local community members in the transformation of public spaces in their community. In the process, the Hack would bypass the existing planning procedures and showcase a new approach to urban planning while uncovering indigenous knowledge.

HACKING TRASH
2017 KUUJJUAQ
HACKATHON

Putting up the flagpole. On the final day of construction, the team considers a finishing touch. *Kuujjuaq, QC*, 2017.

Hanging out in the skating shelter. Young players get set for winter.
Kuujjuaq, QC, 2017.

THE 2017 KUUJJUAQ HACKATHON

This chapter describes and examines the planning processes required to facilitate the Kuujjuaq Hackathon. It summarizes the key elements of our working methodology and presents a blueprint which can be used to organize future community building projects. We look to the differences between plans and experience, to improve the public realm, to reduce landfill waste, and to encourage design exchange. The Hackathon demonstrated that the collaborative design of public space can improve the quality of life of a community and provide an opportunity to rethink waste. It was a collaborative effort by over 60 participants from the Northern Village of Kuujjuaq and an interdisciplinary design team from southern Quebec. Organized by McGill's Minimum Cost Housing Group and the Northern Village of Kuujjuaq, the event leveraged limited resources and limitless talent to reimagine prominent public spaces. The project's driving objectives included; (1) Apply a hacking mindset towards the creation of a thoughtful intervention that positively contributes to the built environment. (2) Creatively explore and repurpose materials that were locally available. (3) Provide a cross cultural collaborative experience and begin important conversations between northern and southern Canadians about design and the built environment in Northern Canada.

PROJECT TIMELINE

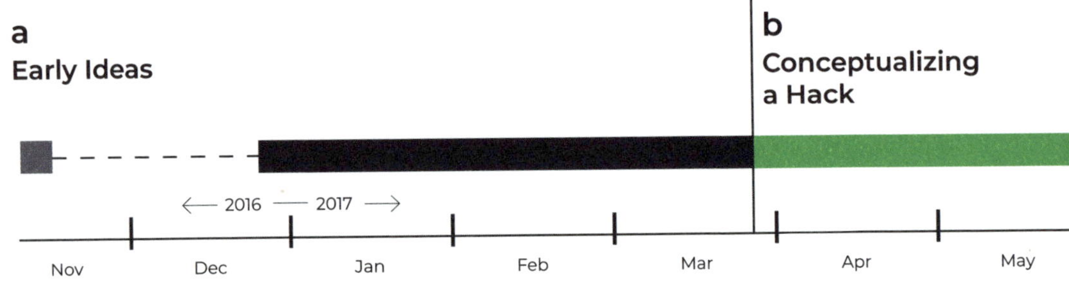

Project timeline: a diagram that depicts the duration of three main phases of the project a) Early Ideas, b) Conceptualizing a Hack, c) Implementing a Hack.

Reassembling the North. 2016 CCA Design Charette.

Event Promotions. Advertising the event on the local radio station and Facebook.

Village Design Sessions. Creating opportunities for co-design.

Collecting Materials.

C
Implementing a Hack

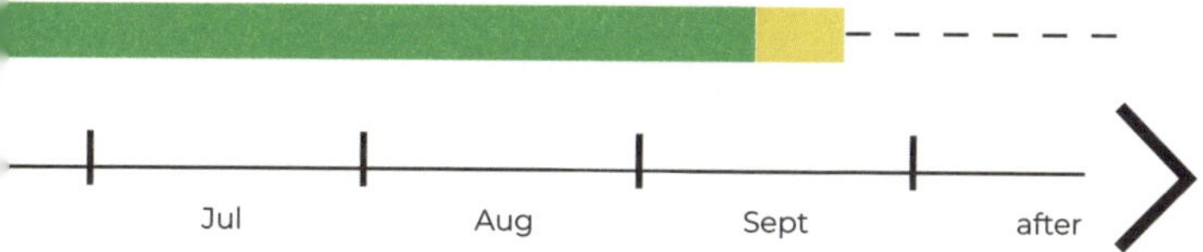

Assembling a Team. Developing a robust team with diverse expertise.

Preliminary Design. Over teleconference calls the team would prepare preliminary design ideas.

Logistics Planning. Working to secure accommodations and affordable airfares.

Repurposing as a Team. Troubleshooting to realize design ideas.

Site Preparations. Preparing the ground for construction.

Re-design and Construction. Mounting the hack.

Partial team photo after the second day of construction.
Kuujjuaq, QC, 2017.

Project Leaders: Vikram Bhatt and Susane Havelka
Project Coordinator: Dave Harlander
Participating designers: Justin Bouttell, Maggie Cabana, Kassanda Bonneville, Emmanuelle Lauzier, Andrée-Anne Caron-Bois-vert, Alexandre Morin, and Flavie Martineau
Community Liaison: Marie-Pierre Macdonald

The Kuujjuaq team included Mayor Tunu Napartuk (Partner), Ron Gordon (Project Coordinator), Mae Ningiuruvik (Administrative Support) and Paul Parsons (Designer). The Montreal team consisted of members from the MCH/HG, the winning charette participants, and a community liaison who had previously worked in Kuujjuaq and for the MCHG.

CONCEPTUALIZING A HACK

June - Sept. 2017

Assembling the Team: Excited by the ideas generated at the 2016 CCA charrette, Kuujjuaq mayor Tunu Napartuk joined McGill's Vikram Bhatt and Susane Havelka to set the Hackathon in motion. They conceived it as a collaborative, multiday design-build event in which a diverse team consisting of members from both southern Quebec and the Northern Village of Kuujjuaq would design and construct an intervention to improve public space. In the spirit of the charette, the event sought to hack key public spaces by creatively repurposing materials from the municipal dump, an existing informal design practice that is commonplace in subarctic and arctic communities. Rather than build one of the charette's winning proposals, the organizing team sought to create an event in which the hacking mindset would be used to design for specific community needs.

In early spring, they recruited David Harlander from McGill University as a project coordinator, to help contribute to the groups search for funding. By mid-March, Habiter le Nord Québécois (HLNQ) provided an important support grant, which helped make this project a reality. Shortly after, Ron Gordon, Kuujjuaq's municipal project manager, was appointed as the teams Kuujjuaq project coordinator. By June 2017, the initial team consisted of 15 core members and was organized in two regional groups. The Kuujjuaq team included Mayor Tunu Napartuk (Partner), Ron Gordon (Project Coordinator), Mae Ningiuruvik (Administrative Support) and Paul Parsons (Designer). The Montreal team consisted of members from the Minimum Cost Housing / Hackathon group, including Vikram Bhatt, David Harlander and Susane Havelka, as well as the winning charette participants including, Justin Bouttell, Maggie Cabana, Kassanda Bonneville, Emmanuelle Lauzier, Andrée-Anne Caron-Bois-vert, Alexandre Morin, Flavie Martineau and a community liaison, Marie-Pierre Macdonald.

Diagram depicting key team members of the Kuujjuaq Hackathon.
See diagram for names and titles.

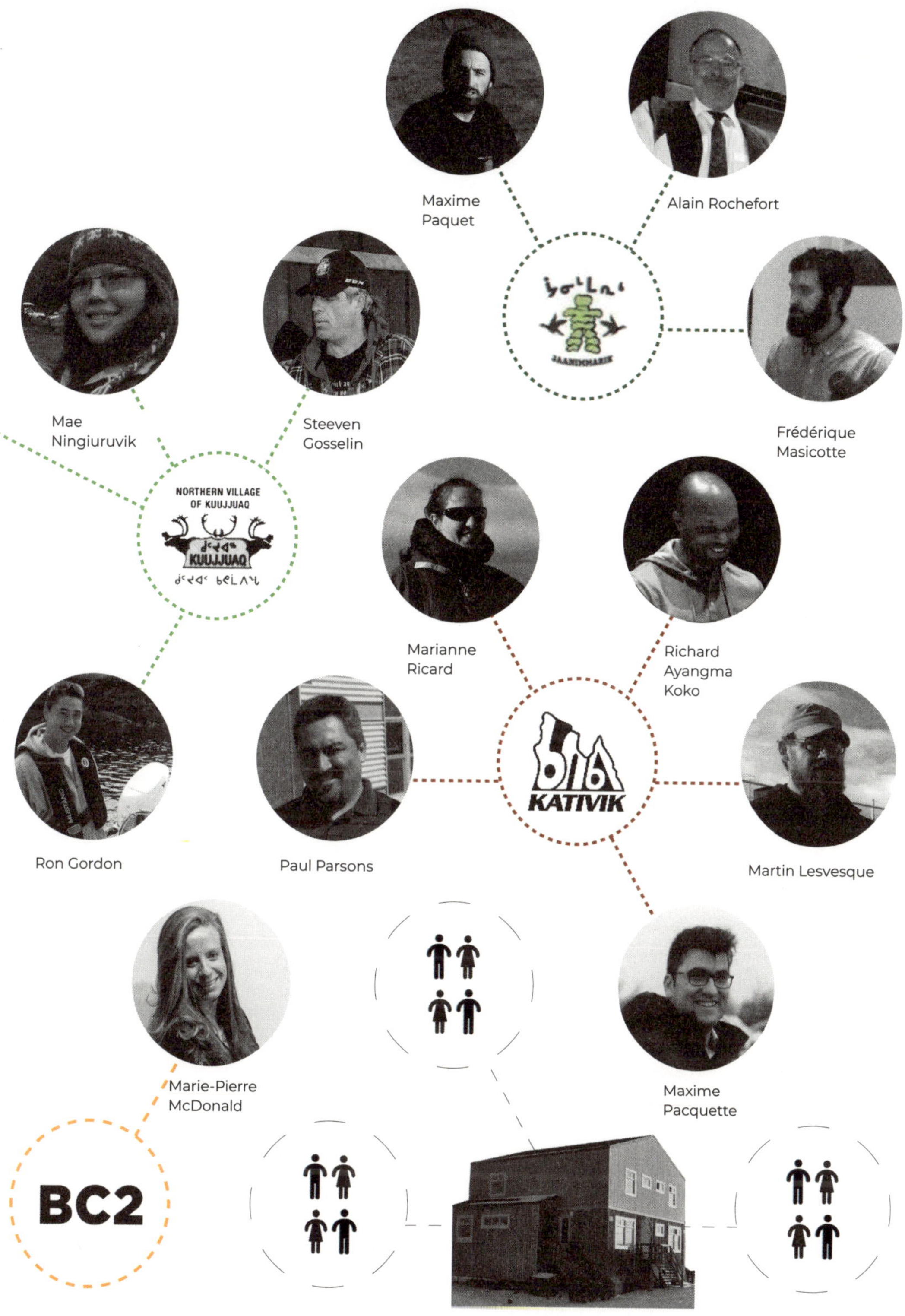
Maxime
Paquet
Alain Rochefort
JAANIMMARIK
Frédérique
Masicotte
Mae
Ningiuruvik
Steeven
Gosselin
NORTHERN VILLAGE
OF KUUJJUAQ
KUUJJUAQ
Marianne
Ricard
Richard
Ayangma
Koko
KATIVIK
Ron Gordon
Paul Parsons
Martin Lesvesque
Marie-Pierre
McDonald
Maxime
Pacquette
BC2

An image of the Hackathon facebook website.

Skype sessions facilitate meeting between northern and southern team members.

DEVELOPING THE PROJECT ITINERARY

June - Sept. 2017

Beginning in June, the geographically separated groups would connect on a weekly basis through Skype sessions. Over the course of these conversations, a preliminary plan emerged. The project would launch with an opening ceremony at the town hall. A series of design sessions would follow. Visits to the village dump were scheduled on the first and third days. First to catalogue available materials and inform the scheduled community design sessions, and secondly to collect and transport materials to the selected project site. The last three days were dedicated to construction and clean up. A closing ceremony with community feast was organized to close the event.

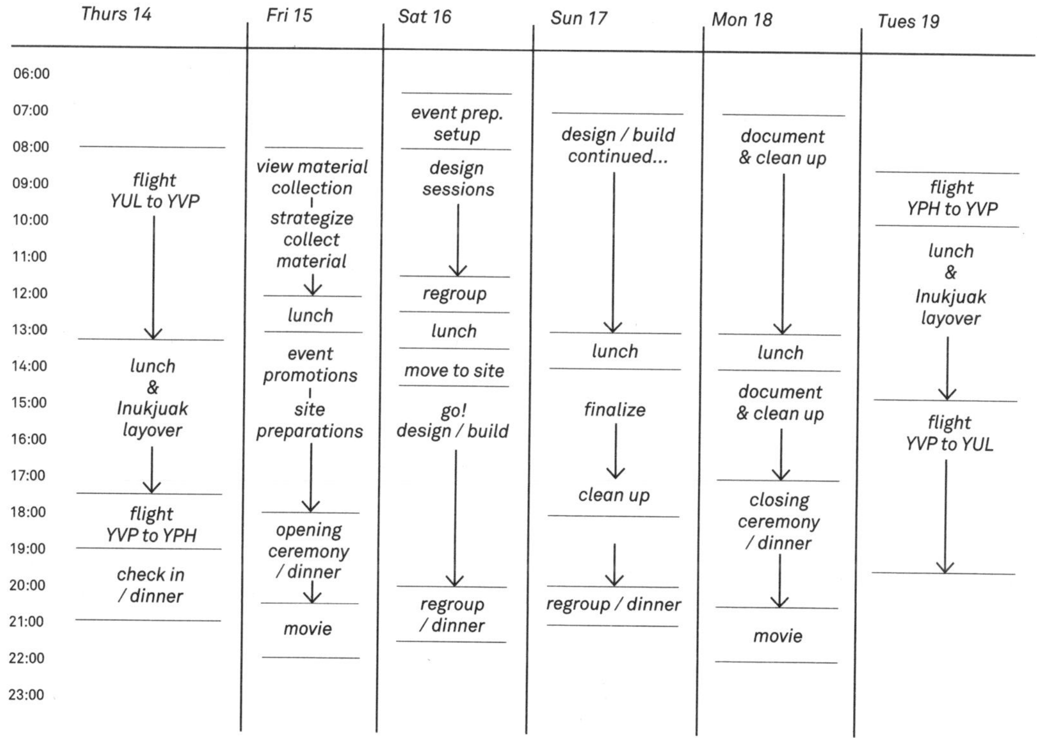

Final draft of the project schedule before departure.

LOGISTICS PLANNING & PROMOTION

June - Sept. 2017

Logistical discussions regarding transport to Kujjuaq and accommodations in the community were also clarified over the summer. The Northern Village of Kuujjuaq had generously offered to lend the community's small school bus to the team, to facilitate transport throughout the village. The village also helped support airfare for the team members with reduced rates normally reserved for Inuit travel rather than the normal airfare. The team was generously hosted in the homes of two different families in the community. This provided a unique opportunity, whereby the project could support local families, and also proved to be a unique living environment for southern team members.

Promotions for the event began in mid-August when a website was created, and used as a platform to promote the event to the community. By the time the event unfolded, it's facebook page had over one hundred followers. Posters were also created and displayed at the town hall and in the schools, promoting the event's opening ceremony and design sessions. A message was also circulated over Kuujjjuaq's Community Radio Station.

Driving to the project site. *Kuujjuaq, QC, 2017.*

The school bus, parked outside the village dump. The bus was lent to the team for the duration of the project. *Kuujjuaq, QC*, 2017.

View of the project site, sent to the Montreal team in August. *Kuujjuaq, QC*, 2017.

DESIGN PREPARATIONS

June - Sept. 2017

Over Skype, the team conducted a series of preliminary design discussions. Kuujjuaq members identified three potential sites and shared images and descriptions. Collective discussions explored each suggestion. Dialogue on available materials also helped stimulate ideas for each site.

Map of Kuujjuaq with three preliminary sites of intervention.

Community design session at the Kuujjuaq town hall. *Kuujjuaq, QC*, 2017.

Drawings from a design session at the Jaanimmarik School. *Kuujjuaq, QC*, 2017.

COMMUNITY DESIGN SESSIONS

June - Sept. 2017

When the team first arrived in Kuujjuaq, an opening ceremony was hosted at the village town hall. A series of public community design sessions soon followed in the next two days, providing opportunities for village residents to participate in the project's design process. Two evening design sessions were held at the community town hall and working design ideas were projected on a large theatre screen.

In addition, short meetings in over 10 classrooms in both primary and elementary schools occurred over two days. While the project's core team already included several Kuujjuaq residents who helped provide insight and drive the project's design objectives, the community design sessions opened up a dialogue about the project to the community at large. Some residents would actively criticize working design proposals and make suggestions of their own, while others would curiously observe the design team at work. Feedback from these events was very insightful, especially with regards to establishing the project goals and the final siting of project. Eventually, a loose design was established to address three interconnected challenges which worked to generate the projects' driving objectives;

Goal 1: Improve the public realm by addressing specific northern needs.
Goal 2: Reduce landfill waste.
Goal 3: Provide collaborative opportunities that facilitate conversations about the public realm in the community.

Discussing design options at the town hall. *Kuujjuaq, QC*, 2017.

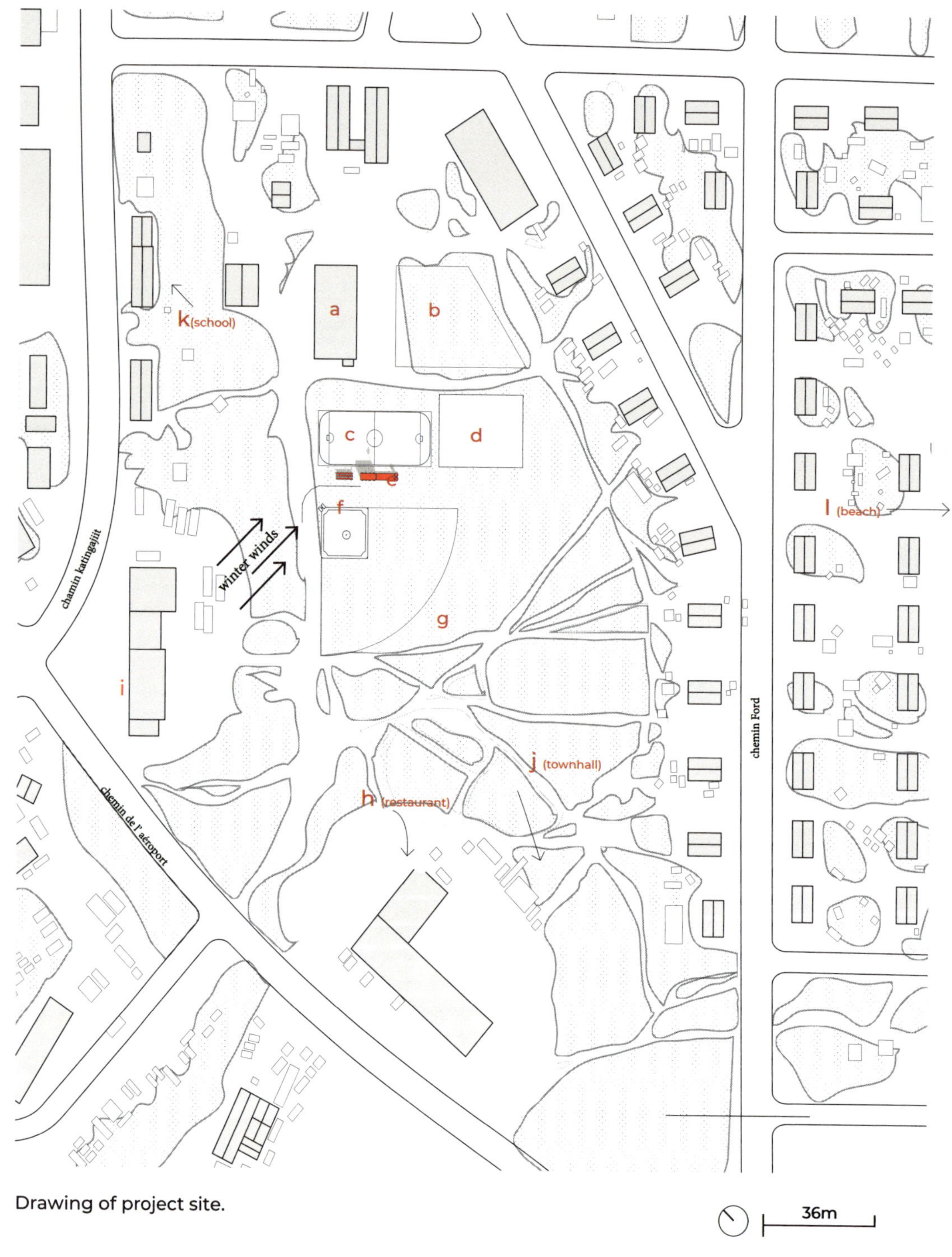

Drawing of project site.

- a workshop (40m)
- b playground (60m)
- c skating rink (2m)
- d skate park (30m)
- e proposal (0m)
- f baseball diamond (2m)
- g field (2m)
- h restaurant (160m)
- i firehall (90m)
- j townhall (330m)
- k school (420m)
- l beach (530m)

PROJECT SITE

June - Sept. 2017

The design team was challenged to activate a large 2.7 hectares recreational open area in the centre of the village. The area's loose rectangular form is defined by four adjacent roadways that parallel the village grid which is rotated 30 degrees from north. A significant elevational increase of approximately 10m defines the NW and SW edges of the site and restricts vehicular access to the area's NE and SE edges. Most of the area consists of recreational fields. To the northeast is an outdoor skating rink, a skate park, children's playground, and a municipal workshop. The sheer size and openness of the area subject it to extensive winds in the winter, predominantly coming from the west. The chosen sight for the design intervention was on a small strip of land 7.5m wide, between three of the most prominent recreational programs of the area; the baseball diamond and the recreational fields to the southwest, and the skating rink to the northeast.

Map of Kuujjuaq, highlighting the project site.

Hackathon site and pavilion as viewed from the firehall parking lot. Letters refer to legend on previous page.

First visit to the project site. *Kuujjuaq, QC*, 2017.

(town hall)
g (field)

COLLECTING MATERIALS

June - Sept. 2017

On the second day of the event, the team made their first visit to the village dump to catalogue available materials. This information fueled community design sessions. Equipped with photos of key objects from the dump, pencils and donuts, conversations began to identify driving criteria for the project. By the third day, a loose design was established and the team was ready to begin collecting materials for construction. With the help of community members, including the municipal dump master Steeven Gosselin, the team began the transport of materials to the site for construction.

Delivering materials to the project site. *Kuujjuaq, QC*, 2017.

Scouting for a sea-canister at the dump. *Kuujjuaq, QC*, 2017.

Collecting the culvert at the dump. *Kuujjuaq, QC*, 2017.

Martin Lévesque collecting septic piping at the dump. *Kuujjuaq, QC*, 2017.

Selecting the right tires. *Kuujjuaq, QC*, 2017.

Loading the flatbed truck with materials. *Kuujjuaq, QC*, 2017.

Loading the pickup truck. *Kuujjuaq, QC*, 2017.

Justin Bouttelle and Flavie Martineau hunting for scrap lumber.
Kuujjuaq, QC, 2017.

Collecting conduit piping.
Kuujjuaq, QC, 2017.

Andre-Anne Caron-Boivert and Kassandra Bonneveville at the Kuujjuaq dump.
Kuujjuaq, QC, 2017.

CONSTRUCTION

June - Sept. 2017

Construction occurred over three days between September 16th and 18th. On the first day of construction, critical design decisions such as the project siting, its programmatic objectives and form had been established. The team split into three groups, one focused on-site preparations and cleaning, another started to disassemble and prepare materials, and the last group worked to finalize important construction details. By the second day, tires, metal septic tanks and found lumber were used to create the foundations of the project. By the third day, the teams refocused, each addressing one of the project's three sections; the dugout, the skating shelter and the stage. A critical project leader involved with all groups was the village dump master Steeven Gosselin, whose enthusiasm for the project and his past DIY construction experience proved very helpful to ensure the project was completed on time.

Discussing the best strategy for mounting the village flag.
Kuujjuaq, QC, 2017.

Building materials unloaded on site.
Kuujjuaq, QC, 2017.

Preparing the ground for tire foundations.
Kuujjuaq, QC, 2017.

Preparing materials for construction, de-nailing, cleaning and sorting. *Kuujjuaq, QC*, 2017.

De-nailing scrap lumber from old shipping crates.
Kuujjuaq, QC, 2017.

Preparing foundations for the dugout.
Kuujjuaq, QC, 2017.

Moving tires. *Kuujjuaq, QC*, 2017.

The tire foundations for the skating shelter. *Kuujjuaq, QC,* 2017.

Filling tire foundations with soil. *Kuujjuaq, QC,* 2017.

Preparing the base for the beacon. *Kuujjuaq, QC,* 2017.

Installing decking on the stage. *Kuujjuaq, QC,* 2017.

Lowering the modified sea-canister onto tire foundations. *Kuujjuaq, QC,* 2017.

Preparing the beacon cap. *Kuujjuaq, QC,* 2017.

Cleaning up the skating shelter.
Kuujjuaq, QC, 2017.

Cleaning up the bleachers.
Kuujjuaq, QC, 2017.

Steeven Gosselin, dump master.
Kuujjuaq, QC, 2017.

Steeven Gosselin helping install the village flag. *Kuujjuaq, QC*, 2017.

Youth relaxing in the skating shelter. *Kuujjuaq, QC*, 2017.

Collage of Hackathon Pavillion.
Kuujjuaq, QC, 2017.

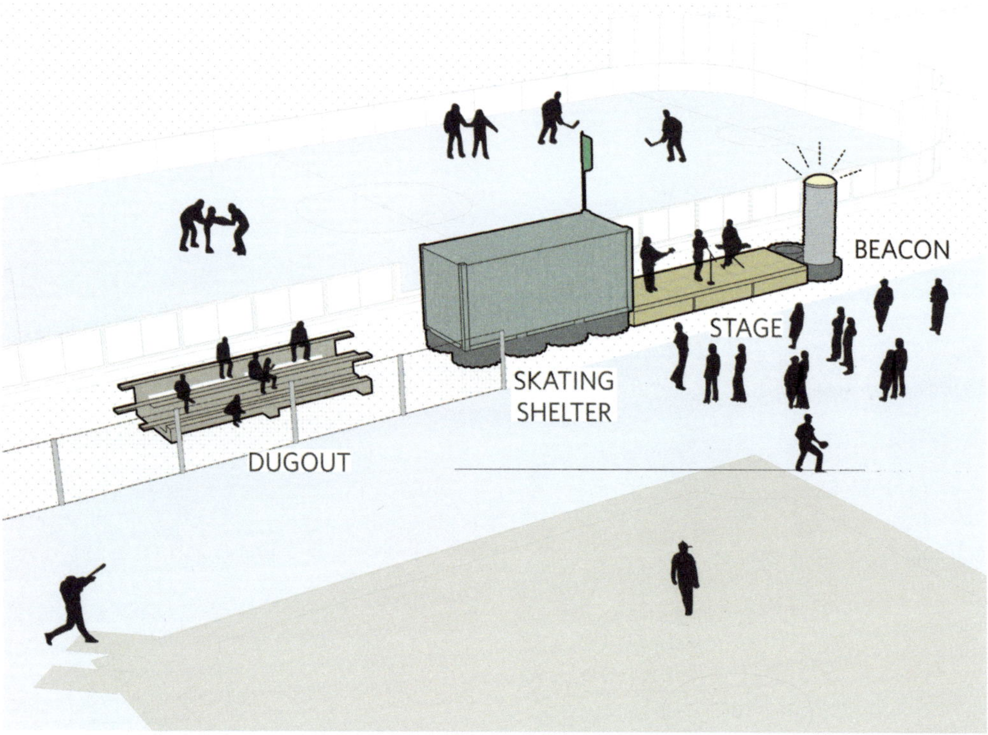

Schematic diagram of the project's programme.

South Elevation.
Kuujjuaq, QC, 2017.

DESIGN CONCEPT

June - Sept. 2017

The proposed design was organized as a simple long bar in four parts. Each part responded to a specific programmatic need related to the adjacent programs of the site. At the far northwestern end is a set of wooden bleachers that serve as a dugout and also provide an elevated view from which to watch a baseball game. A 3m pathway separates these bleachers from the project's second element: a skating shelter. It is made of an opened sea container placed on a base of eight giant tractor tires. It is oriented towards the skating rink to the north east and strategically blocks prevailing winter winds. Beside the skating shelter lies a 2.3m x 7m stage used for community events such as outdoor music concerts or presentations. The stage is framed with a beacon made of a metal culvert that is topped off with an old recycled PVC skylight and equipped with a car battery operated light. This vertical element provides light at night, announcing evening concerts.

THE PAVILION

The four programmatic elements of the pavilion consisted of a dugout for viewing baseball games, a wind shelter for skaters to give shelter from harsh and penetrating winds, a stage for outdoor performances and a light beacon to illuminate the space at night.

Young community members come by to see the project on the last day of construction. *Kuujjuaq, QC*, 2017.

Dugout: The dugout was constructed from 2" x 12" lumber pieces which were initially attached to building debris and full of rusty nails. Much time was spent de-nailing and cleaning up these boards before they could be safely handled and used.

Skating Shelter: Tractor tires were filled with sand and used as the foundations for the skating shelter made of an opened sea container. Found lumber was used to provide a bench at the back of the structure. Ski-doo tracks were used to provide a slip resistant floor.

Stage: Three metal septic tanks were used as the foundation for the stage. A decking system was constructed from lumber and plywood from used shipping pallets.

Light Beacon: Two large tractor tires were placed at the end of the stage and filled with sand. At the southeastern end of the project a 3m tall culvert with a PVC sky-light was mounted to provide a light beacon and help frame the stage.

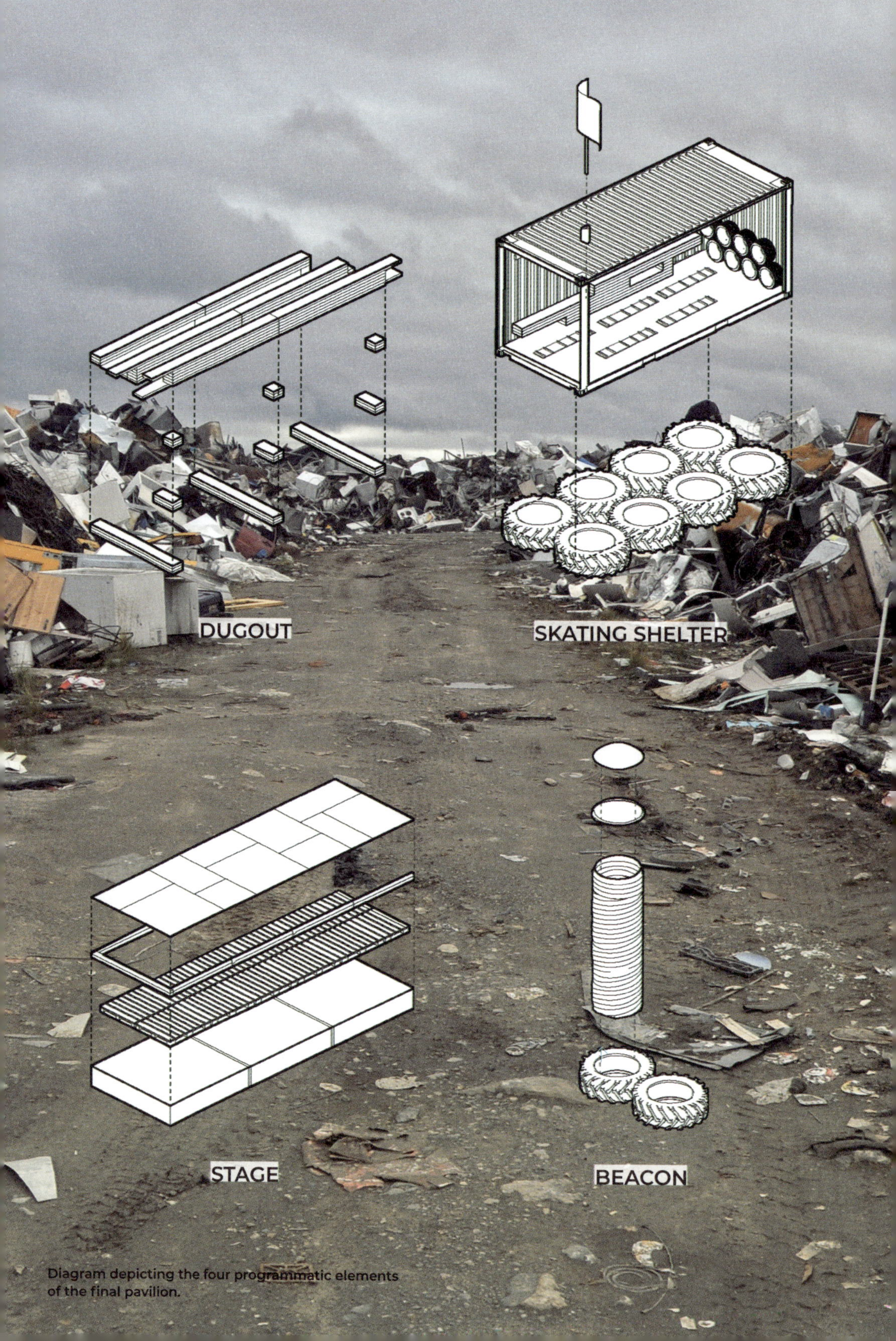

DUGOUT

SKATING SHELTER

STAGE

BEACON

Diagram depicting the four programmatic elements of the final pavilion.

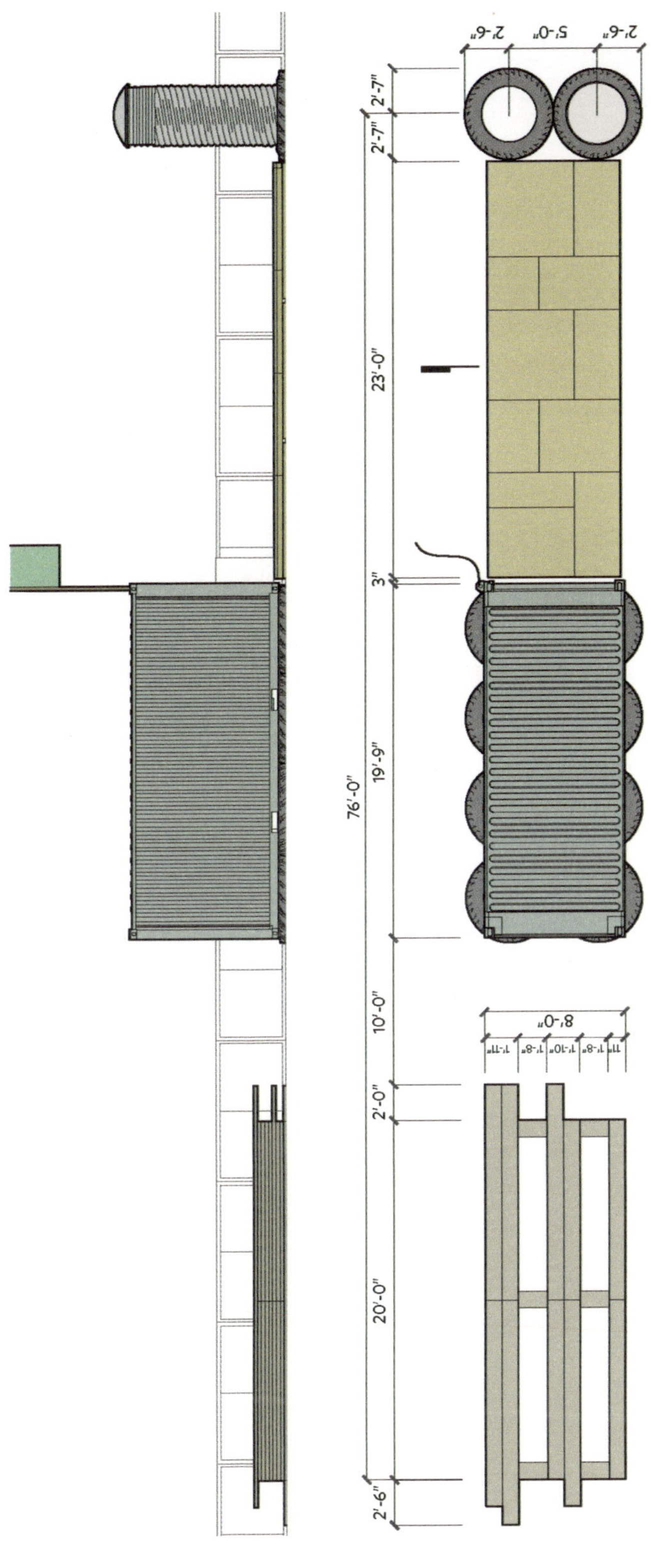

Drawings of the southwest elevation and plan.

Southeast view of the skating shelter from the skating rink. *Kuujjuaq, QC*, 2017.

Northwest view of the skating shelter from the stage. *Kuujjuaq, QC*, 2017.

Perspective of the skating shelter from the firehall parking lot. *Kuujjuaq, QC*, 2017.

Ice skaters in Kuujjuaq can now take refuge from Nunavik's cold in this unique shelter designed by the community and its help from a group of designers who helped organize the hack. It is important to note that this unique design-build process only saw formal drawings emerge after the project was built. Throughout construction, sketches, notes and rough models were used to design, communicate and facilitate building.

CONCLUSION

Jaanimmarik School students arriving at the pavilion for outdoor recreation. *Kuujjuaq, QC*, 2017.

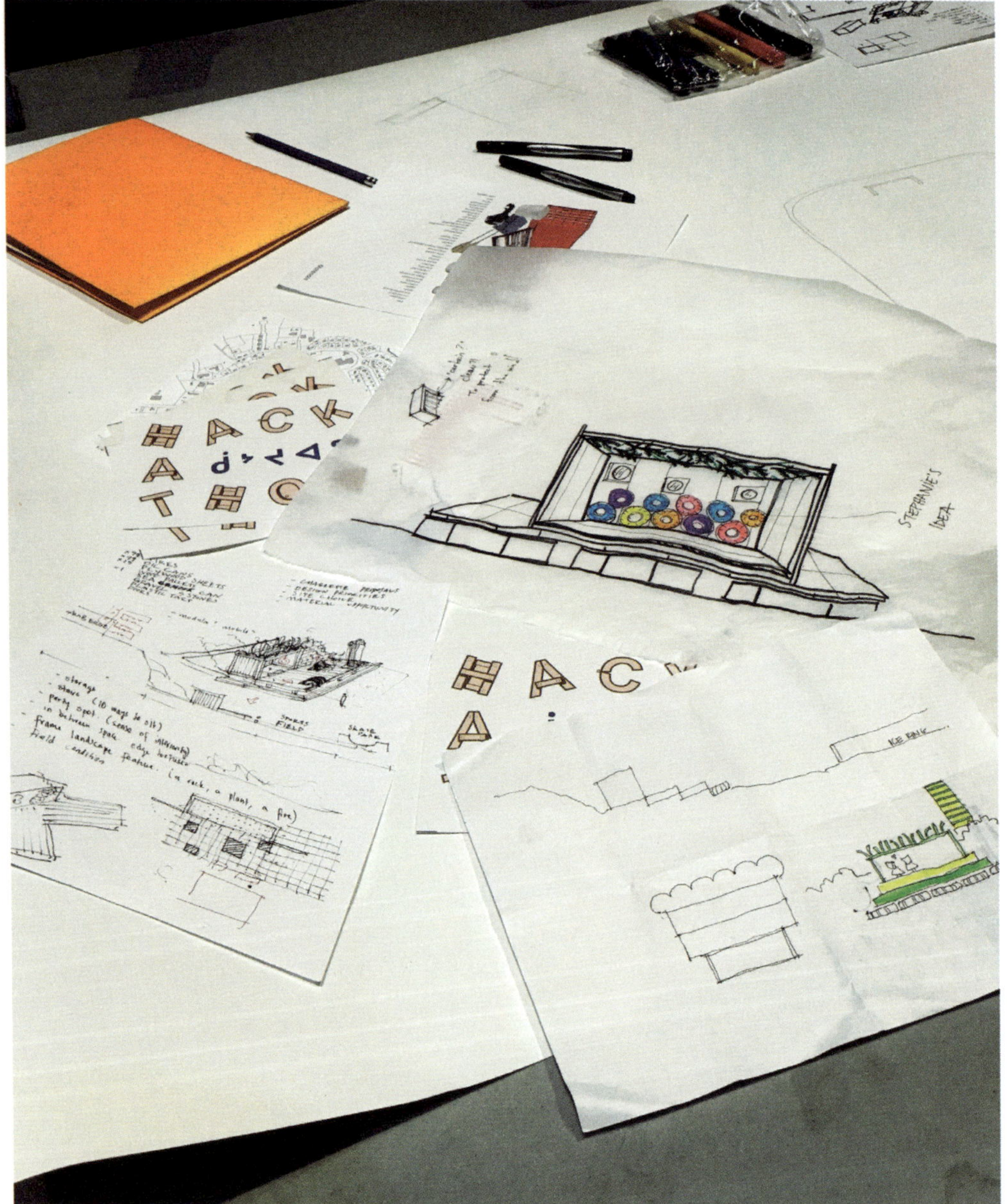

Drawings produced at the town hall community design session. *Kuujjuaq, QC*, 2017.

BLUEPRINT FOR A HACK

The CCA Charrette and Hackathon worked in tandem. Young designers' putting forth ideas within a skillfully framed design charrette generated a wide range of ideas and a creative range of solutions. This in turn served as an inspiration for the Hackathon, which would later be recognized by the Royal Architectural Institute of Canada, the Canadian Institute of Planners, and the Canadian Society of Landscape Architects with the 2018 National Urban Design Award in the Small or Medium Community Urban Design category.

The event also allowed a variety of people to participate – experts and professionals. Local partners were essential to the process. Tools like Google photos and maps were invaluable as they helped provide important contextual information to the design team in Montreal. Other key elements include forethought and planning, background research and a platform for public engagement, including digital outreach through social media.

The five day Hackathon was the culmination of a long gestation period. What we did up front through Skype included; Brainstorm potential design ideas, preliminary site selection (final selection in the field) and promote the event to the community. These elements were paramount to the project's success.

Installing the village flag. A view of the pavilion from the skating rink.
Kuujjuaq, QC, 2017.

FILLING THE PLANNING GAP

Designers often overlook outdoor public space. The few public structures that exist in the North tend to be copied from southern models with no attempt to address specific northern needs. Take, for example, Kuujjuaq's outdoor hockey rink. Set upon an expansive open field, the rink is subject to biting winter winds – yet offers no designated shelter for patrons to lace up and store boots. That leaves users to lace up in their pickup trucks. Residents without a vehicle rarely use the rink. In summertime, baseball players also lack safe storage for valuables. The Hackathon reimagined these centrally located public spaces. The built intervention was an unprecedented example of community-based design that addressed specific needs. Importantly, the project also sparked conversations about the built environment and how the community can take charge of it.

View of the Kuujjuaq dump with the tires in foreground and the Koksoak River in the distance. *Kuujjuaq, QC*, 2017.

REDUCING LANDFILL WASTE

Waste management problems may be exaggerated in the remote context of Kuujjuaq, but they also affect societies everywhere, including southern Canada. DIY hacking culture can effectively address a global need for designers to reconsider the second life of building materials and design interventions to reduce waste, and rethink consumption patterns. *Anything from snow to earth when available in large quantities can become building materials. Why not our waste?* This project capitalized on the North's strong DIY building culture and showcased its relevance as a design approach that can recover, reduce, and recycle waste materials and help rethink our consumption patterns.

Preparing the ground for tire foundations. *Kuujjuaq, QC*, 2017.

COUNTERING THE STATUS QUO

Hacks most often target an abstract concept such as bureaucracy, or political correctness. In Inuit communities, Hacking is the logical reaction to dysfunctional housing bureaucracies. They provide important responses to many of the inadequacies of existing government housing.

As “occupy and self-build” architecture, the Hackathon challenges current planning norms and regulations.

Self-built cabin outside of town. *Kuujjuaq, QC*, 2017.

A NEW ARCHITECTURAL PARADIGM

Rooted in successful informal building practices The Kuujjuaq Hackathon showcased a creative working method that brought together material and human resources from Kuujjuaq to reclaim and reshape some of the village's forgotten public spaces. Events like the CCA charrette and Hackathon underscore the importance of community participation in planning and design processes. In their book *Ephemeral Urbanism*, Rahul Mehotra and Felipe Verde argue that "ephemerality challenges us to develop tools for intervening and thinking about nonpermanent configurations as a legitimate category within the discourse on urbanism" (Mehrotra et al. 2017). Not only in seasonal and episodic events but in all kinds of urban settings, including in the northern context, we need better tools. No doubt formal space producing disciplines have much to contribute. But their potential will always be limited without the cooperation, even leadership, of local stakeholders.

Mehrotra, Rahul, Felipe Vera, José Mayoral, Richard Sennett, and Richard Burdett. *Ephemeral Urbanism: Does Permanence Matter?*, 2017. Print

Taking a break on the last day of construction. *Kuujjuaq, QC*, 2017.

HOCKEY

“When you first approached us, we were somewhat confused with your terminology. What exactly was ‘hacking’? But as you explained just what you were trying to do, we reacted ‘Ahh, ok. I know what you are saying. We do that all the time.”

Tunu Napartuk

Modifying tractor tires for the base of the light beacon. *Kuujjuaq, QC*, 2017

INTERVIEW WITH A HACKER

Two years after the Kuujjuaq Hackathon, David Harlander spoke with Tunu Napartuk to gather his thoughts on the event and its legacy. He discovered the hacking mindset and approach to informal building remain decidedly present in the community – and its former mayor.

DH: So much has happened in two years. Can you remember first hearing about the idea?

TN: Definitely. When [previous mayor] Paul Parsons first introduced me to the project, I wasn't certain what to expect. But when you described it to me, I instantly got the concept. What you call 'hacking' is something we do all the time. As Inuit living in a remote region, with limited resources, we must reuse all available materials and reimagine new possibilities for the kind of stuff that is normally considered waste in places like southern Quebec. Once I understood what you were proposing, I did not hesitate to connect with Vikram and the Minimum Cost Housing Group. It was so easy to work with everyone.

DH: One thing that stood out for me during the event was how the people of Kuujjuaq so easily took on leadership roles. Key team members like Ron Gordon [project manager at the NV of Kuujjuaq] and Steeven Gosselin [Kuujjuaq's dump master] had such a natural understanding of how to achieve the project's design goals – how to cut open a sea canister, the right type of tires to be used as the pavilion's foundations, where to find them, how to move them and so on. They led all of us.

TN: I recently had a conversation with a friend about the ingenuity of our ancestors. We discussed how they had to make do with what they had – literally living off the land. Historically, there was little technology, there was no metal or wood to build with. Most communities in northern Quebec don't even have trees. So, they made snow houses, they built knives with bones and driftwood, they invented the Qayaq, what you call the kayak.
When you sit back and consider the environment they contended with – the same environment we live in today

Installing the light beacon and stage decking Kuujjuaq. *Kuujjuaq, QC*, 2017.

– you must tip your hat to my ancestors' ingenuity. And they did it all with plenty of humor! It's quite special.

DH: Another thing that struck me was the tremendous enthusiasm during the design sessions at Jaanimmarik School. Do you think similar "hands on" design activities could be a good fit for future curriculum programming?

TN: We have so much potential. And we now realize how ingenious Inuit are. We don't need titles like "scientist" or "doctor", or the education that this modern society requires to gain status. Still, given all the changes in our society over the last 60 years, we Inuit are trying to find our identity. Having small hacks like that – reusing what we have – lets us showcase our skills. I'm certain the young students would identify with programs that use this concept.

DH: That is certainly the sense we had throughout the Hackathon. Have you noticed a change in DIY building projects in the years since the event? People always hacked, but do you think the event raised awareness of the idea?

TN: Not necessarily. As I mentioned, recreating and reusing what we have has always been with us. If you just walk around town, you'll see it in the shacks, you'll see it in the cabins on the outskirts of the community. Someone stuck on the land with a broken snow machine doesn't always have all the tools and materials needed to fix it. But time and again they get by. These are the kind of hacks I see every day.

DH: I heard you are building your own cabin. Would you tell me about it?

TN: Yes, I'm building my own cabin. It is 16"x 24" and made from plywood and 2X4s. It has one room and a spare space for storage. It's just outside the community, a 15-minute drive from my home. I'm not much of a carpenter but luckily many friends are very good, natural carpenters. They helped me out a lot. My kids will have their space. They will be able to run around it.

DH: Sounds exciting and again speaks to the strong culture of DIY building in Kuujjuaq.

Self-built cabin on the outskirts of Kuujjuaq. *Kuujjuaq, QC*, 2017.

TN: Yes, this do-it-yourself approach is an inspired way to involve the community, including the youth, in local building processes that leverage limited resources, but it cannot however be considered a cure to the impoverished living standards we currently face; it is important to properly fund and source the housing and material needs. Inuit have much to be proud of. Our culture, values and traditions work for us. With all the changes we've experienced in such a very short time, we seem to have gotten away from that. We must step back from our current modern ways and appreciate the hard work of our ancestors and the cultural values they developed. We should take more pride in it all. And we do.

November 2019

Jumping off the stage. *Kuujjuaq, QC*, 2017.

LIST OF IMAGES

Pages 96 - 97
- Hanging out in the skating shelter. Young players get set for winter. *Kuujjuaq, QC, 2017.* photo: Emmanuelle Lauzier

Pages 98 - 99
- Reassembling the North. 2016 design charette. *Kuujjuaq, QC, 2016.* photo: Vikram Bhatt
- Event promotions, the project's facebook page. photo: David Harlander
- Assembling a Team. *Kuujjuaq, QC, 2017.* photo: Susane Havelka
- Preliminary Design. *Kuujjuaq, QC, 2017.* photo: Marie-Pierre McDonald
- Logistics Planning. *Kuujjuaq, QC, 2017.* photo: Marie-Pierre McDonald
- Community Design Sessions. *Kuujjuaq, QC, 2017.* photo: Marie-Pierre McDonald
- Collecting Materials. *Kuujjuaq, QC, 2017.* photo: Susane Havelka
- Site Preparations. *Kuujjuaq, QC, 2017.* photo: David Harlander
- Design and Construction. *Kuujjuaq, QC, 2017.* photo: David Harlander

Pages 100 - 101
- Partial team photo after the second day of construction. *Kuujjuaq, QC, 2017.* photo: Marie-Pierre McDonald

Pages 104 - 105
- Skype sessions facilitate meetings between northern and southern team members. *Montréal, QC, 2017.* photo: Marie-Pierre McDonald

Pages 106 - 107
- Driving to the project site. *Kuujjuaq, QC, 2017.* photo: Maggie Cabana
- The school bus, parked outside the village dump. The bus was lent to the team for the duration of the project. *Kuujjuaq, QC, 2017.* photo: André-Anne Caron-Boisvert

Pages 108 - 109
- View of the project site, sent to the Montreal team in August. *Kuujjuaq, QC, 2017.* photo: Andrée-Anne Caron-Boisvert

Pages 110 - 111
- Community design session at the Kuujjuaq town hall. *Kuujjuaq, QC, 2017.* photo: Susane Havelka
- Drawings from a design session at the Jaanimmarik School. *Kuujjuaq, QC, 2017.* photo: David Harlander

Pages 112 - 113
- Discussing design options at the town hall. *Kuujjuaq, QC, 2017.* photo: Justin Bouttell

Pages 116 - 117
- First visit to the project site. *Kuujjuaq, QC, 2017.* photo: David Harlander

Pages 118 - 119
- Delivering materials to the project site. *Kuujjuaq, QC, 2017.* photo: Emannuelle Lauzier

Pages 120 - 121
- Scouting for a sea-canister at the dump. *Kuujjuaq, QC, 2017.* photo: David Harlander
- Collecting the culvert at the dump. *Kuujjuaq, QC, 2017.* photo: Susane Havelka
- Martin Lévesque collecting septic piping at the dump. *Kuujjuaq, QC, 2017.* photo: Susane Havelka
- Selecting the right tires. *Kuujjuaq, QC, 2017.* photo: Kassandra Bonneville
- Loading the flatbed truck with materials. *Kuujjuaq, QC, 2017.* photo: Susane Havelka
- Loading the pickup truck. *Kuujjuaq, QC, 2017.* photo: Susane Havelka
- Collecting conduit piping. *Kuujjuaq, QC, 2017.* photo: Emannuelle Lauzier
- Justin Bouttell and Flavie Martineau hunting for scrap lumber. *Kuujjuaq, QC, 2017.* photo: Susane Havelka

Pages 122 - 123
- Andre-Anne Caron-Boivert and Kassandra Bonneveville at the Kuujjuaq dump. *Kuujjuaq, QC, 2017.* photo: Maggie Cabana

Pages 124 - 125
- Discussing the best strategy for mounting the village flag. *Kuujjuaq, QC, 2017.* photo: Emannuelle Lauzier

Pages 126 - 127
- Building materials unloaded on site. *Kuujjuaq, QC, 2017.* photo: Andre-Anne Caron-Boisvert
- Preparing the ground for tire foundations. *Kuujjuaq, QC, 2017.* photo: Susane Havelka
- Preparing materials for construction, de-nailing, cleaning and sorting. *Kuujjuaq, QC, 2017.* photo: Emannuelle Lauzier
- De-nailing scrap lumber from old shipping crates. *Kuujjuaq, QC, 2017.* photo: Susane Havelka
- Preparing foundations for the dugout. *Kuujjuaq, QC, 2017.* photo: Maggie Cabana
- Moving tires. *Kuujjuaq, QC, 2017.* photo: Maggie Cabana
- The tire foundations for the skating shelter. *Kuujjuaq, QC, 2017.* photo: Maggie Cabana
- Filling tire foundations with soil. *Kuujjuaq, QC, 2017.* photo: Susane Havelka
- Preparing the base for the beacon. *Kuujjuaq, QC, 2017.* photo: Andre-Anne Caron-Boisvert
- Installing decking on the stage. *Kuujjuaq, QC, 2017.* photo: Maggie Cabana
- Lowering the modified sea-canister onto tire foundations. *Kuujjuaq, QC, 2017.* photo: Maggie Cabana
- Preparing the beacon cap. *Kuujjuaq, QC, 2017.* photo: Susane Havelka

Pages 128 - 129
- Cleaning up the skating shelter. *Kuujjuaq, QC, 2017.* photo: Emannuelle Lauzier
- Cleaning up the bleachers. *Kuujjuaq, QC, 2017.* photo: Susane Havelka
- Steeven Gosselin, dump master. *Kuujjuaq, QC, 2017.* photo: Maggie Cabana

Pages 130 - 131
- Steeven Gosselin helping install the village flag. *Kuujjuaq, QC, 2017.* photo: Marie-Pierre McDonald
- Youth relaxing in the skating shelter. *Kuujjuaq, QC, 2017.* photo: Marie-Pierre McDonald

Pages 132 - 133
- Collage of the Hackathon Pavilion. *Kuujjuaq, QC, 2017.* photo: David Harlander

Pages 134 -135
- South Elevation. *Kuujjuaq, QC, 2017.* photo: David Harlander

Page 136 - 137
- Young community members come by to see the project on the last day of construction. *Kuujjuaq, QC, 2017.* photo: David Harlander

Pages 140 - 141
- Southeast view of the skating shelter from the skating rink. *Kuujjuaq, QC, 2017.* photo: Louis Babin-St-Jean
- Northwest view of the skating shelter from the stage. *Kuujjuaq, QC, 2017.* photo: Louis Babin-St-Jean

Pages 142 - 143
- Perspective of the skating shelter from the firehall parking lot. *Kuujjuaq, QC, 2017.* photo: Justin Bouttell

LIST OF FIGURES

Pages 84 - 85
- An image from the charrette entry "*Ecran*". source: Canadian Centre for Architecture, 2016.

Pages 86 - 87
- An image from the charrette entry titled "*This is Not a Threshold*". source: Canadian Centre for Architecture, 2016.
- Diagrams from the charrette entry "This is Not a Threshold". source: Canadian Centre for Architecture, 2016.

Pages 88 - 89
- Image from *Hacking Workshops - Ateliers* charrette entry. source: Canadian Centre for Architecture, 2016.

Pages 90 -91
- Poster created to promote the Hackathon event.

Pages 98 - 99
Project timeline: a diagram that depicts the duration of three main phases of the project *a) early ideas, b) Conceptualizing a hack, c) implementing an Hack.*

Pages 102 - 103
- Diagram depicting key team members of the Kuujjuaq Hackathon. See diagram for names and titles.

Pages 104 - 105
- An image of the Hackathon Facebook website.
- Final draft of the project schedule before departure.

Page2 108 - 109
- Map of Kuujjuaq with three preliminary sites of intervention. source: Northern Village of Kuujjuaq

Pages 114 - 115
- Drawing of project site. source: Northern Village of Kuujjuaq (contours), Justin Bouttell (drawing).
- Map of Kuujjuaq, highlighting the project site. source: Northern Village of Kuujjuaq (base map).

Pages 116 - 117
- Hackathon site and pavilion as viewed from the firehall parking lot. Letters refer to legend on previous page.

Pages 134 - 135
- Schematic diagram of the project's programme

Pages 138 - 139
-Diagram depicting the four programmatic elements of the final pavilion.
- Drawings of the southwest elevation and plan.

REFERENCES

Debarbieux, Bernard. «Béatrice COLLIGNON, Les Inuit: ce qu´ ils savent du territoire, Paris, L´ Harmattan, 1996, 254 pages.» *Cybergeo: European Journal of Geography* (1998).

Duhaime, Gérard, Sébastien Lévesque, and Andrée Caron. "Nunavik in figures 2015 – full version." *Québec: Canada Research Chair on Comparative Aboriginal Condition, Université Laval* (2015): 133.

Havelka, Susane. *Building with IQ (Inuit Qaujimajatuqangit): The rise of a hybrid design tradition in Canada's Eastern Arctic*. Diss. McGill University, 2018.
"Kuujjuaq Village Map." *Nunavik Landholdings Corporation*, 2016.
"Kuujjuaq Zoning map." Katikik Regional Government, 2017.
Mehrotra, Rahul, Felipe Vera, José Mayoral, Richard Sennett, and Richard Burdett. *Ephemeral Urbanism: Does Permanence Matter?*, 2017. Print.

Nunavut Eastern Arctic Shipping Inc. . *NEAS Sailing Schedule. NEAS Sailing Schedule*, 2017. https://neas.ca/wp-content/uploads/sailing_schedule.pdf

Peter Jacobs, Daniel Berrouard and Paul Mireille. "Nunavik: A homeland in transition." *Kuujjuaq, Kativik Environmental Quality Commission.* http://www. keqc-cqek. ca/KEQC-AR09-eF-lo. Pdf (2009).

Pete Seeger. Lyrics to "*if It Can't Be Reduced." 2008*

"Reassembling the North / Recomposer le Nord - Inter-university Charrette.", Canadian Centre for Architecture, 2016.

Renewable Resources, Environment, Lands and Parks, et al. "Nunavik Residual Materials Management Plan." *Nunavik Residual Materials Management Plan* , 2015. www.krg.ca/ images/stories/docs/ Environment/ PGMR_Eng.pdf.

THE AUTHORS

Vikram Bhatt, M.Arch. FRAIC, FRSC

Vikram Bhatt, is an internationally recognized expert in the field of sustainable housing and human settlements design. A graduate of CEPT University (1973), India, where he also worked with Pritzker Laureate Balkrishna Doshi. Following which, he obtained his graduate education in housing at the McGill University, School of Architecture; where currently, he is a Professor Emeritus, and Director, Minimum Cost Housing Group (MCHG). MCHG focuses on the global shelter problems of poor dealing with issues of human settlements planning, urban design and housing via action-research and creative interactive engagements – charrette, hacks and community partnerships. Vikram is a recipient of numerous awards, including the prestigious AD Research Award (1990), Graham Foundation for the Arts Fellowships (1993 and 2000), RAIC National Urban Design Awards (2008 and 2019), and Margolese National Design for Living Prize (2014) for outstanding contributions to the development or improvement of living environments for Canadians of all economic classes. His pioneering work on edible landscapes and urban agriculture has focused on food security and successfully transformed neighborhoods and cities around the globe improving lives of ordinary people. As the co-creator of the 21st annual inter-university charrette, Reassembling the North and the 2017 Kuujjuaq Hackathon, Vikram has also helped advance important conversations about the role of design in remote northern communities of Canada. His work has been disseminated widely and his publications, in particular, *After the Masters*, co-authored with Peter Scriver, and *Resorts of the Raj*, represent high levels of achievement in new and important areas of architectural scholarship

David Harlander, M.Arch

David holds a professional Master's of Architecture from the University of British Columbia and a post-professional Master's of Urban Design and Housing from McGill University. His research explores housing and community development in Northern Canada and has seen him contribute to projects based in the Yukon, Northwest Territories and Nunavik. His work has received various accolades, including the Cornelia & Peter Oberlander Prize in Urban Design, the Louis B. Magil Fellowship in Housing and the Norbert Schoenauer and David Farley Fellowship in Architecture, among others. As part of the Minimum Cost Housing Group (MCHG), he played a leading role in the award-winning 2017 Kuujuaq Hackathon. In addition to his continued involvement with the MCHG, he currently works at an architectural office in Montréal.

Susane Havelka, Ph.D.

Susane is currently a postdoctoral research fellow at Memorial University of Newfoundland. Her research interests lie at the intersection of housing, community engagement and user-generated cold-climate building techniques. Dr. Havelka's doctoral thesis, completed at McGill University, investigates the rapid rise of a hybrid architectural design practice in Canada's Eastern Arctic. Building on the success of the 21st Annual inter-university Charrette, she co-created the award-winning 2017 Kuujjuaq Hackathon. She studied science, art and design at MIT and Architecture at Columbia University. After completing her master's degree, Susane practiced as an architect in New York, Berlin and Prague before undertaking a doctorate at McGill University. During this time, and inspired by her friends in Nunavut and at the Monolithic Dome Institute, she designed and tested a self-build prototype as an innovative building system for extreme climates and remote northern communities. Susane now divides her time between conducting research on housing and well-being in Arctic and sub-Arctic communities and developing an experimental cluster of dome houses as the first working project "dadaDome" in an Arctic region. She hopes to enable Inuit to design and build affordably and autonomously using local materials, simple techniques and the internet to share designs and ideas.

Group photo after the third day of construction. *Kuujjuaq, QC*, 2017.

Dedicated to the Northern Village of Kuujjuaq